Becoming a Mother:
The First Six Weeks

Becoming a Mother: The First Six Weeks

An Essential Guidebook for

New Mothers

Magbule Doko, M. D.

I dedicate this book to my daughters and to all the women who soon will begin their journey into Motherhood

This book is intended to be a guide to early motherhood. This book does not replace the advice of your physician.

Table of Contents

Preface

The best gift I received at my baby shower was not a cute little onesie or tiny baby shoes, it was a small handbook that my sister made for me. It was titled "From One New Mother to Another". During the first six weeks of motherhood I read that book perhaps 30 times. During that hectic time, her book kept me grounded. It saved me so many times when I was feeling inadequate in my new role. It reminded me that being a mother was hard, but the best thing I could ever experience. It reminded me that my engorged breasts would not stay that way forever. It reminded me that this tiny human being was my responsibility. It reminded me that I had to be strong for my baby.

I want to share what I learned during those first six weeks. Before having my baby, I read lots of information about newborn care and the postpartum period. At the time, two of my sisters were mothers and even they did not give me a truthful version of what becoming a new mother would entail. Being a doctor, I thought that maybe I would be more prepared for this job. However, all my medical knowledge did not help me when I had to change diapers in the middle of the night, give my newborn a bath, and process all the emotions associated with postpartum blues.

I want to thank my husband, Drilon, for all his support while I was writing this book. Your endless support means so much to me.

I hope that by writing this book, I can help mothers-to-be and parents-to-be have a better idea of how the first six weeks will be. I am going to write about all the things that I wish someone had told me. I will try to add in the medical perspective of things throughout the book. I hope that this book offers you the information and inspiration you need during your journey to becoming a mother.

Being a mother is undeniably the best job in the world.

Welcome Baby

There are lots of books out there about pregnancy and labour and all of them offer plenty of information. I encourage you to read books about pregnancy and labour so that you are better prepared and knowledgeable on the subject. So, instead of repeating what those books say, I want to tell you my pregnancy story and my experience with labour, delivery, and the first moments with my new little one.

The day I found out I was pregnant was one of the happiest days of my life. I had invited my family over to celebrate New Year's Eve. I had the turkey ready, the vegetables cut, and the soup simmering. My husband was working and would be home late in the afternoon. We had been trying to get pregnant for some time and I was expecting my period sometime this week. I really don't know why, but I had a feeling that I should do a pregnancy test that day. I was prepared. I had tests that I had ordered online, I had the ones from the drugstore, and I had bought some digital ones just to make sure. I was always nervous before doing one of these tests because whenever it showed up negative my heart would break all over again. Although I was very stressed during the time that we were trying, my husband was very calm and maintained a positive attitude. He would say, "It will happen when it's meant to happen". He would offer me words of encouragement and hope. He will always be my rock in this life. Back to the story – so there I was, waiting the two-minute wait that felt like a century. Two pink lines! Pregnant! Really?! I double-checked with the digital test and it read "1-2 weeks pregnant" (which really meant 2-4 weeks according to how us doctors calculate it). How can I describe the feeling that I felt? I was floating on clouds. I felt out of my body. I was so happy. I was afraid that my happiness would make the sun shine even brighter at that moment. Was it real? Is it true? I have a little human being growing inside me? Looking down at my tummy I couldn't believe it. It didn't look any different than yesterday. I was ecstatic, thrilled, excited, and full of joy. I needed to tell my husband! I decided I would wait until he gets home from work, but I wanted to make it a nice surprise. I went out to the store and bought some pink and blue blocks that had the word "baby" on them and wrapped them up. I also had the pregnancy tests ready to show him. He came home around 5 pm and I told him I wanted to give him his New Year gift. I don't know how I was holding back my excitement. I gave him the gift. He was a bit confused and then I gave him the digital pregnancy test and he yelled out "You are pregnant!". It was the best moment for us as a couple. That little human being was making us go crazy in that moment. We already loved it so much, more than anything. I said to him "this is the best gift ever!"

I was so thrilled to be pregnant! Seeing all those pregnant patients, I always wondered how it would be like for me. Doing numerous newborn examinations made me always wonder how would I hold *my own* baby?

People say that being a doctor is beneficial at times of illness. This is true since as doctors we have an understanding about diseases. We know what tests should be done and what medicine should be given. However, it's also a disadvantage. We always know everything that can go wrong. So, for me, that thrill of being pregnant immediately turned to anxiety. I could only hope that everything would go fine. I can say that I did have a baseline anxiety for the nine months of pregnancy and during the labour. When I finally heard my baby girl's first cry, I took a deep breath and relaxed, well, for a little bit.

My first trimester was a difficult one. I was doing a rotation in General Surgery and I had not told my supervisor or residency program director yet. I had symptoms of extreme fatigue and dizziness at times. Being on my feet all day in the operating room was getting harder to do. I tried to stay hydrated and I would wear my knee-high compression stockings. One morning, there was a case where they were going to be using a special chemical that required the use of x-rays. I didn't want to expose my little one to x-rays so I had to find a way to get out of that surgery. Luckily, we had a medical student working with us. So, I told him my news and he covered for me in that surgery case. Later, during my rotation in Student Health, morning sickness settled in. It was so bad I had to excuse myself from a patient's room once to take a deep breath and eat something. My nausea would be relieved by food. I had to always make sure I had snacks on me, such as, snack bars, fruits, and nuts. Therefore, I gained too much weight in the first trimester! Once the second trimester came around, my nausea had settled.

You know how they say the second trimester is the best? It was for me. No more morning sickness and I started showing. I also felt the baby move, which was truly amazing. We took advantage of an upcoming holiday and told our families. We chose to wait until the second trimester to tell our families. Being a doctor, I knew about the risk of miscarriage in the first trimester and I did not want to be in the situation where I give good news and then give bad news to my family. We told our news to a small circle in the beginning so that we have some support during the first trimester. When making the decision about when to tell your news, just remember that miscarriage is more likely in the first trimester.

Now, in my second trimester, I had more clinical rotations to complete. I completed my rotations in palliative care, geriatrics, and OB/GYN (obstetrics/gynecology). My OB/GYN rotation was very fulfilling for me at that time since I could empathize with patients now that I was pregnant. My patients would see my belly and ask me how I was feeling. They seemed happy to be seeing a pregnant doctor. We were all in the same boat. Delivering babies on the rotation made me worry about how my own experience was going to be. That baseline anxiety increased in severity as my due date neared.

The third trimester hit and hit me with a bang. I had just started my second year of family medicine residency. I completed one week and then started to notice pain in my right lower back. I ignored it at first, thinking it was just because I was on my feet too much. As days went by, the pain got worse. If I would stand, I would get a severe pain in my lower back to the point that I could not stand anymore. I went to work the next day, another 12-hour workday in the office, and came home almost falling to my knees from the pain. I had right-sided sacroiliitis. That means that I had inflammation in my right joint between the sacrum and iliac bone. I needed to be off my feet and wear a sacroiliac belt all day. I could only take acetaminophen for the pain since any anti-inflammatories may be dangerous for the baby. So, I made the decision to start my maternity leave two months before my due date.

In addition to my back pain, I was then diagnosed with gestational diabetes. I had counselled many patients about this disease but now I can say that I truly understand what the patient goes through. I was monitored closely and had to follow a strict diabetic diet. My sugar levels were not high enough for insulin, but my endocrinologist said that they may increase to the point where I may require insulin. I could not accept that I had to prick my finger four times a day. The first time the diabetes team nurse showed me how to do it, I almost cried because I could not believe that I was given this diagnosis. Eventually, all the sugar testing skin pricks became second nature to me.

The pregnancy kept challenging me, but I stayed strong. I also had a large support network. My number one support was my husband. You need your partner on your team during the pregnancy. The pregnancy is the easy part, the delivery is the medium-hard part, but the most difficult part comes after that baby is born. That is when your team should be the strongest. Get your partner reading the pregnancy books, take them to prenatal classes, and include them in your baby preparation. My husband and I went to prenatal classes at our local public health unit. They were free nightly classes, once a week for six weeks. I initially thought to myself that we were going to the classes more for the benefit of my partner. Since I was a doctor, I knew all that baby stuff, right? Wrong. I learned a lot about baby care and about what to expect. During my time at home waiting for baby to arrive, I kept myself updated in my medical field by reading research articles. I also started my preparation for my Family Medicine Board exams. My sister, who had a five-month old baby at home, helped me with the baby preparation. She helped me prepare the room and buy all the essentials. I decided to do spring cleaning too before the baby came. This was hard to do being nine months pregnant, so I recruited some help. I had my little sister and brother sleepover and persuaded them to help me. So, we got all the cleaning done and then enjoyed a movie and popcorn.

I also took care of all the maternity leave forms before the baby came. I had to complete a form for the hospital I worked for and for the government in order to receive benefits. I was planning on taking one year off for maternity leave. My residency program allowed me to do this. Once I would be finished residency, I would not have the luxury of taking one year off. I would have my own family practice and I would have patients that are my responsibility. So, either I would need to find someone to work for me and run my office or I would have to go back to work. Once I completed everything on my "To Do Before Baby Arrives" list, I was ready to meet my baby and start being a mother.

The day finally came. My water broke in the early hours one night. My hospital bag was more like my hospital luggage. I didn't have any contractions initially. I had planned to see how things would go and then ask for the epidural if I thought I needed it. Most of my patients that would come to the labour floor also had this plan but most of the time they ended up getting the epidural. I ultimately decided to get it since my contractions at that point were eight out of ten severity and I could not imagine them getting worse. Even with my epidural, I could still tell when my contractions were occurring. It was comforting to know that I still could feel them. My sister and my husband were with me for the labour and delivery. They were so supportive, getting me ice chips, placing a cool towel on my forehead, and helping me breathe through my contractions. Before I knew it, it was delivery time. We were going to meet our baby soon! The doctors and nurses were all set up. The neonatal nurses were present also and ready to check the baby. I don't know why, but when I felt a contraction I would say "are you guys ready'" to the doctor and nurses. The doctor said to me "yes we are ready, are YOU ready"? Yes, I was. Before I knew it, I heard my baby's cry and gave her a big kiss. We had become parents and I could say that I was truly happy. Quoting Chris Rock's character from the popular comedy movie "What to Expect When You Are Expecting" (based on the famous pregnancy book by Heidi Murkoff), "I used to think I was happy, now, I know that I'm happy". The character was explaining how he felt after having children.

After my baby was born, the obstetrician continued managing the delivery of the placenta and I got to hold my baby girl. My baby's cry was the most amazing sound I had ever heard in my life. I was crying and laughing at the same time. I could not believe that I did it and I could not believe that I was looking at a completely new human being. My husband and I gave her a big kiss and my sister captured that moment in a beautiful photograph. *True love*. The love for your child is a true love. Yes, you love your parents and siblings. Of course, you love your partner. However, the love for your child is a different love. It is absolute true love. From that moment I was in love. I love all my children the same. They are an extension of myself. No matter what type of day I have been having, one look at my children and I am happy. My husband always says to people "Have you seen the biggest diamonds in this world?" and they reply "No, of course not", and he says, "They are right here!" and he points to our children!

The nurses helped me to start breastfeeding my daughter within the first hour of birth, which is the recommendation. My new baby just knew what to do. I am not saying breastfeeding was easy because with my first child it was not. I think it all depends on the personality of the baby. Even today, my first child is a picky eater and she was difficult to breastfeed. I will get more into this in the *Feeding* chapter. They moved us to our private room and I got to freshen up a bit. After that, we called our families and gave them the news. They were at the hospital in no time to see the new baby and I. When I saw my mother, she came and kissed me on the cheek and we looked at each other and started crying. We didn't have to say it. We both knew. I had entered motherhood. I had gone through what she had gone through eight times. My mother had eight children. Her firstborn, which she had at the age of 18, passed away from gastroenteritis and dehydration at six months old. The passing of this child still gives her a deep ache. She was living in Eastern Europe at the time, where they did not have a good healthcare system. She went on to have seven more children and I fit in as number two. Essentially the "oldest". I remember my mother raising us in an effortless manner. It seemed so natural to her. We always feel her love everywhere we go.

The family visitors left, and my husband and I were alone in the hospital room with this small new life. Our responsibility. Weight on our shoulders. Parenting is a huge responsibility and a huge privilege. A privilege to be able to raise another human being. We were new at this, but we were ready. So, that first night, the baby woke up every two hours to breastfeed and required a diaper change at every feeding. The change in sleep pattern was exhausting. Don't worry if you are a heavy sleeper. That baby will wake you up! That is why they have such a loud cry. Your body will get used to the sleep pattern with time. The next day, we had more visitors essentially at all the times when we had to sleep. By the afternoon, the doctor had cleared us to go home. So, we started packing our things and let the family know that we were leaving the hospital. I nominated the nurse that helped me during my labour for the Daisy Award, an award that recognizes exemplary nurses, and she won! I wanted her to be praised for her hard work and excellent care. The doctors and staff were excellent, and I thank them all.

Before you leave the hospital, there is a newborn screening test that is performed by taking a blood sample from the baby's heel. This newborn screening checks for over 20 different genetic disorders. It is a standard test done on all newborns in Ontario, Canada. Also, the baby will get a hearing test done before leaving the hospital. Other standard medical treatments include a Vitamin K injection to prevent a bleeding disorder called hemorrhagic disease of the newborn. Erythromycin ointment is also placed in each of the newborn's eyes to help treat any gonorrhea or chlamydia microbes that the baby may have been in contact with in the vaginal canal. If the baby gets these microbes in their eyes it could lead to blindness. Also, bloodwork is done on the baby to check its bilirubin level. This is a chemical that can be dangerous to the baby's brain if the level is too high. If bilirubin is too high, then the baby is said to have jaundice. Some babies require phototherapy to help decrease the amount of bilirubin in their blood. Each baby also gets a physical exam before leaving the hospital. In different areas of the world there may be additional or different tests or medical treatments that are given to newborns before leaving the hospital.

The first day home with your new baby is special. You are welcoming your child into your home. You are becoming a family (or extending your family if you have other children). So, don't forget to take pictures and record video if you can. **Cherish those first moments with your new baby**. So, my husband and family took all the bags, gifts, and balloons down to the car. The baby was dressed in her going home outfit that we handpicked for her. I keep this home outfit in her memory box now. As we walked out of the hospital with her, I felt a feeling of completion – as if one part of my life was over and I was beginning a new part. The part where *I am a mother and we are a family*. A new chapter.

That moment when we walked through the door with our baby was a special moment. Welcome home baby! Our families were there, and they all held the baby and then baby and I moved into the bedroom. We had the crib set up beside our bed in our bedroom. This is called co-sleeping, which is different from co-bedding. In the *Sleeping* chapter we will go through sleeping recommendations. We settled the baby in new pyjamas and went through one breastfeeding and diaper change cycle. Then back to sleep for baby. Remember to take those precious photographs and video of your newborn baby.

Family and friends will have an opinion on the way you are raising your baby. Just say "Thank you, I will consider that" and you do what feels right for your baby. **You are the mother and you will have that *Lioness instinct* to protect your child and take care of it.** It is an instinct for a reason! So that you *do* protect that child. So, **listen to your instinct** and remember you have been given a *great privilege* by being given this baby. We will talk more about this instinct later. Don't forget that as new parents, things will get frustrating. This is normal! You both are suddenly given new roles. New jobs with no prior training. **Parenting is training on the job.**

I hope that this book gives you some insight into what is to come. Remember, a new baby is coming, and you need to be prepared to take care of that tiny, precious human being. Let me help you by guiding you through the early weeks of motherhood.

The Essentials

The Essentials chapter will be just about that. It will be about the *pure Essentials* you will need for yourself and for your baby. We will also go through some essential Things *to Do Before Baby Comes*, essential *Hospital List*, and packing the baby bag. At the end of this book, you will have a complete checklist and you can use it to check off items.

Part 1: Essential Baby List

Every baby needs an essential amount of clothing, diapers, bathing products, feeding products, equipment, and all those miscellaneous products.

Essential Baby Clothing

First, let's talk about sizes. You will find that each company will size the clothing differently. So, one company's newborn size clothing may or may not match with another company's newborn size. **A newborn, by definition, is an infant between 0-28 days old**. Use your own baby's size and visual cue to decide if a piece of clothing will fit your baby and do not rely on the clothing label.

Baby skin is very sensitive, especially newborn skin. Some babies that eventually may have eczema, an inflammatory skin condition, may show signs of it early on. So, I suggest buying **clothing cleaning products that are dye-free, fragrance-free, or made for sensitive skin**. Another thing I found helpful was, if you can, **washing the baby clothing in a separate load** from the older children or adult loads. So, this way, any chemicals or products on the other clothing do not seep into the baby clothing and cause skin problems. In addition, **if you own a dishwasher consider buying hypoallergenic dishwasher liquid or tabs**. Allergies are more common in children that have a dishwasher in the home, especially if the dishwasher liquid or tabs or not hypoallergenic. We will talk about cleaning bottles in the *Feeding* chapter.

As I list the essential clothing, I may add comments about an item. I use ten as the essential number because that means you go through two a day roughly and by day five you will be likely washing a load of baby clothes. The more of each item you have, the less loads you will be washing a week.

- ☐ 10 Short sleeve onesies

- ☐ 10 Long sleeve onesies

- ☐ 10 Pyjamas – These can be snap up, zip up, or two piece. Remember, **babies need one extra layer than us at any given time**. This rule is not hard and fast. If you are outside on a hot summer day (preferably in the shade to protect baby), you will not put on two layers on your baby. Zip up pyjamas are great, but you must be careful with the end of the zipper. Make sure it is pointing down and not towards the baby's neck. Two-piece sets are convenient because it is easier to change a diaper with them. However, you must make sure the top part is tucked into the bottom, so your baby's back does not get cold. Snap up pyjamas are the easiest to work with.

☐ 1 Pyjama sack (aka Pyjama bag, swaddling sack) – Pyjama sacks are great products. Why? At bedtime, you can place your baby in the pyjama sack and you do not have to use a blanket. The recommendation is that you should not place anything loose in the crib. No pillows, no blankets, no padding, and no stuffed animals. We will talk more about this in the *Sleeping*

Chapter. The best products would be the pyjama sacks that also swaddle the baby. Swaddling is the term given to a certain method of wrapping the baby so that the blanket is tight around the baby. **This tightness mimics the womb setting and helps to calm and settle the baby.** It also helps them sleep better. Some swaddling sacks even come with Velcro so it is easy to swaddle the baby. *This product is a must!*

☐ 10 Pants

☐ 10 Sweaters – This may not apply if you have your baby in springtime or summer. Wool sweaters may irritate the baby's skin.

☐ 1-2 Hats – Hats are very cute on babies, especially if you are outside with your baby and it is chilly. However, inside the home or at bedtime, do not put a hat on your baby. **Babies release heat from the top of their heads**. So, even if you overdress your baby because you are not sure how many layers to put on, the baby has a venting system! It will release that extra heat through its head!

☐ 3 Hand Mittens – These you will need because **you should not clip your baby's nails until they are at least 4 weeks old**. There is risk of damaging the nail or fingertip, so it is better to wait. Hand covers keep the baby from scratching their face.

☐ 5 pairs of Socks

☐ 4 Swaddle Blankets – these are the thin blankets that you can swaddle the baby with.

☐ 2 Blankets

☐ Baby laundry basket

☐ Baby memory box (and/or book) – you will need someplace for all your keepsakes

Essential Changing Items

You will need at least one box of newborn diapers to have at home before the baby comes. Then purchase more diapers as needed. Babies outgrow diaper sizes at different times. My babies always wore the next size up before their cousins did. How will you know that it is time to go to the new diaper size? Well, two things – one, you will begin to struggle to put on the diaper. The tabs on the sides will be harder to bring around to the front of the baby. Second, the baby's poop or urine will come out of the diaper and stain the clothing. Then, it's time to move on up the diaper ladder.

☐ One box of newborn diapers and Size 1 diapers – Alternatives to disposable diapers are reusable diapers.

☐ One box of baby wipes – A note here. Standard baby wipes have lots of chemicals on them to make them the way they are. I did find that in the newborn period the baby's skin is very sensitive, so it may redden with use of baby wipes. What I would do is **rinse the wipes with lots of water** and this helped tremendously. I also wanted to mention that there is a product called a wipe warmer. I used it for my children. I found that if I had to change a diaper in the middle of the night, as soon as I put that cold wipe on their bottom, they would cry and then become fully awake. So, a warm wipe will let your baby sleep while you finish changing that diaper. An alternative to baby wipes are reusable baby towels or rags. They do also sell hypoallergenic/natural/organic baby wipes, and these did not turn my baby's bum red as much as the standard baby wipes.

☐ Diaper cream – One large container and a small one for the baby bag. Again, there are different products out there. Basically, you want to purchase one that has a **high level of zinc oxide** in it (average 10%).

☐ Baby changing pad – All those pictures of nurseries tell you that you need a baby change table in the baby room. However, a baby change table is great until the baby starts rolling and moving and then there is risk of falling off the change table. Some babies start rolling at 2 months old. The stores sell baby changing pads that you can put on any surface and change your baby quickly and safely. Once your baby starts moving, which may be as early as two months, I recommend **placing them on the floor to change them**. It is the safest way.

☐ Diaper Light – with one of my children, I had to do many diaper changes in the night. Instead of putting on the room light, I used a small nightlight that had easy on/off switch. Mine was battery operated so I could bring it close to the baby and take a closer look at the diaper situation at hand. My husband and I called this the "diaper light".

☐ Diaper trash – if it has a lid on it, it will work! I kept mine in the bathroom. If the diaper was a poopy diaper, I would put that in a bag first and then throw it into the diaper trash. Another option for the poopy diapers is to keep a small trash container (that has a lid) on the patio/in the garage/on the balcony and throw all the poopy diapers in there.

☐ Laundry detergent – keep a small travel bottle full in your nearest washroom. You will need it to help wash any stains on the baby clothes. **The sooner you wash a stain, the easier it will be to remove.**

Essential Bathing Items

☐ Baby Bathtub – There are different ones to purchase. There are some that come with a bath support for a newborn baby. These are great because newborn babies are slippery when wet!

☐ Baby shampoo/body wash – All baby shampoo/body wash products are made for baby's sensitive skin. The best products are the ones with most natural ingredients. I urge you to read the ingredient list and compare different products. Even a mild bar soap that is perfume free would do fine.

☐ 1 Baby towel

☐ Small jug for rinsing

☐ Bath thermometer – A bath thermometer can help you make sure the bath water is the right temperature for your baby.

Essential Feeding Items

☐ 10 Burping Towels

☐ 10 Bibs – These you can use early on if you have a baby that is spitting up a lot. The bib can help prevent the milk going onto the baby's neck.

☐ Bottles – how many you purchase depends on if you are planning on breastfeeding or not. If you are formula feeding, then you will need 3-5 bottles. If you are breastfeeding, I would still buy at least two bottles. Why? Well, if you need to go out of the house for any reason, you can pump (we will talk all about this later) and that can be given to the baby by bottle. Make sure the nipple of the bottle is for a newborn or 0-3 months old.

☐ Formula – ready made or powdered – 1 package. Even if you plan on breastfeeding, I recommend having some at home for that first week until your milk fully comes in. I have had experiences where I fed my newborn baby but then they would keep on crying. I would try other things to soothe my baby but sometimes they wanted a little bit more to drink that my breasts just did not have at that moment. So, I fed them formula and then off to sleep they went. If you can, buy ready made formula as it will be easier and faster to use in the newborn period. We will talk about this in the *Feeding* chapter.

Essential Equipment

☐ Stroller

☐ Car seat +/- Car seat base – if the weather is cold when your baby is born, you can buy a car seat cover to keep the baby warm when you go outside

☐ Crib + Crib Mattress + Crib Fitted Sheet +/ Crib Waterproof Sheet

☐ High Chair – this you can start using once baby is old enough to sit on his/her own (around 6-8 months).

☐ Baby monitor – good old-fashioned sound monitors will do the job just right.

Essential Medical Items

☐ Thermometer – invest in a good thermometer as you will use it frequently. When your child is sick, you want to know if they have a fever or not.

☐ Infants Acetaminophen or Ibuprofen – have 1 bottle at home ready. You do not want to drive in the middle of the night to the drugstore. **Note that any baby less than 3 months who has a fever must be examined by a physician**.

☐ Antiseptic – rubbing alcohol or hydrogen peroxide. If your baby gets hurt, you need something to clean the wound. I recommend hydrogen peroxide because rubbing alcohol is painful when applied.

☐ Bandages

☐ Antibiotic cream – they sell these over the counter

☐ Vitamin D – they sell as drops or liquid. **If you are breastfeeding, then you need to supplement your baby with Vitamin D** (400 or 600 IU dose). Formula has vitamin D added into the product.

Essential Miscellaneous Items

☐ Baby Diaper/Travel Bag

☐ Tissue box for the room

☐ Small waste basket for the room

☐ 4 Pacifiers – **Pacifiers help soothe a crying or uncomfortable baby**. There is lots of debate about pacifiers, mainly about how using it in the first 4 weeks can cause nipple confusion and then your baby may not breastfeed effectively. For my first child, I did not give her the pacifier until she was 6 weeks old. Both the baby and I suffered through hours of crying that most likely would have been quickly relieved if I gave her a pacifier. With my second child, I used the pacifier from day one and I think we both had a better experience. Make sure you purchase pacifiers for 0-3 months old.

☐ Baby grooming kit – you mainly need the nail cutter, nail file, and soft brush

☐ Nightlight for room

☐ Hypoallergenic laundry supplies and/or dishwasher supplies

☐ Small Bedside Box – you can place some diapers, wipes, diaper cream, and nursing pads in it for easy access.

Essential Baby Diaper Bag Items

The diaper bag or also known as travel bag is an essential baby item when going out with your new little one. You don't want to be caught without a diaper or without a pacifier – especially when you are out. I recommend even leaving extra diapers, wipes, and a pacifier in the car! **I recommend looking through your diaper bag once a week and re-stock as necessary**. This essential list is for the first six weeks with your baby. As your baby grows, the items in your travel bag will change.

☐ Clothing – 2 changes of clothing, 1 pyjama set, 1 pair socks, 1 pair of hand mittens, 1 hat

☐ Diapers – 10 diapers – newborns have frequent diaper changes, so you don't want to run out, especially when you are out of the house.

☐ Diaper Disposal Bags – they sell very nice scented bags so if you must throw away a dirty diaper at a guest's house then the bathroom will not get too stinky.

- [ ] Portable Baby changing pad – there are some diaper bags that come with this.

- [ ] Diaper Wipes – 1 box

- [ ] Diaper cream – 1 small container

- [ ] Baby Wash – 1 small bottle – in case you need to wash your baby's bum after a diaper change

- [ ] Burp Towels and Bibs

- [ ] Pacifier – keep one as a back-up. Some stores sell containers for pacifier storage or use a plastic/Ziploc bag.

- [ ] Bottle – keep one in your diaper bag as a back-up bottle.

- [ ] Formula – 1 can (ready-made or powder)

☐ Extra Tissue

☐ Medical Items: Antibiotic Cream, Bandages, Acetaminophen or Ibuprofen for infants

Part 2: Essentials for You

I will be writing the *Essentials for You* list assuming that you are breastfeeding. If you are not breastfeeding, then disregard those items.

☐ 6 week supply of sanitary pads

☐ Prenatal vitamins

☐ Acetaminophen and Ibuprofen

☐ Stool softener +/- Laxative

☐ Nursing bra – 2 – try to buy ones without a wire as they are more comfortable.

☐ Nursing pads – try different brands until you find one that you like.

☐ Lanolin cream

☐ Nursing pillow +/ nursing pillow cover

☐ Breast pump – Manual pumps work very well. There are electronic pumps out there also. We will talk about this in the *Feeding* chapter.

☐ Breastmilk storage bags

☐ Ice Pack – for perineum and breast care.

☐ Peri-Bottle – aka "Squirt bottle" for rinsing the perineum after childbirth. Most hospitals will have them and let you take it home.

Part 3: Essential Things to Do Before Baby Arrives

☐ Make sure you have the Essentials mentioned above!

☐ Organize baby clothes – organize by type of clothing so they are easier to find. I bought some plastic containers with no top and used these on a bookshelf. Now, if you had a baby shower then you may have clothing for when your baby is older too. I recommend washing the newborn and the 0-3 month old clothing. **Once baby comes, you will be very busy, so do it sooner rather than later**.

☐ Bottles – wash and sterilize them. Sterilize bottles by first washing them with soap and warm water and then putting them into boiling water for at least 5 minutes. At the stores, bottle warmers and sterilizers are sold, however, they are not essential but can help make formula/bottle feeding more efficient.

☐ Spring Cleaning – I recommend cleaning your living space before baby comes.

☐ House to Do List – if there are any home renovations or projects that you have had on your mind, it is always good to do them before baby comes as you will have your hands full with the new baby.

☐ Crib & Car Seat Base installation – have these installed at least 1 month before your due date.

☐ Room setup – you may choose to co-room with your baby. That means you sleep in the same room. This is recommended for at least 6 months. We talk about this more in the *Sleeping* Chapter. Have your crib set-up with the clothing storage area. Have your bedside box ready. Make sure you have everything setup in the room for baby at least one month before the due date.

☐ Charge the camcorder and camera – make sure they are ready for that special day! Buy some extra memory cards or empty the ones you have. Consider buying a back-up hard drive for all those photographs and videos you will be taking of your little one.

☐ Partner & Family Talk – have a sit-down with your partner about expectations once the baby is born. Talk about parental duties, visitors, and couple time. If you have older children, tell them what to expect and how they can help.

☐ Couple time – once the baby is born there will be less couple time. Try to fit in some date nights before baby comes. Some couples go on a "babymoon" vacation before baby comes (check airline regulations regarding flying while pregnant).

☐ Maternity benefits – make sure you have filed all the correct paperwork. Ask your employer for details.

☐ Insurance and Legal Documents – remember after baby is born you should add them to your health/private insurance plans and to any legal documents, such as wills, that you may have.

☐ CPR (Cardiopulmonary Resuscitation) and First Aid Course – Consider taking a local course so you have knowledge of what to do in case of an emergency. Anybody else who will be taking care of the baby can take the course also.

Part 4: Essential Hospital List

Getting ready for that big day is exciting! Below, find a list of all the essentials you will need to bring to the hospital – for yourself, baby, and your partner/birth-partner. Have the hospital bags packed at least one month before the due date.

Hospital Essentials for Baby

☐ Short sleeve onesies, long sleeve onesies, pyjamas – 3 of each

☐ Baby Going Home Outfit – something cute and special for baby's first trip home

☐ Swaddle blanket and blanket – 1 blanket and 4 swaddle blankets -you will need extra swaddle blankets to cushion the baby in the car seat

☐ Hat, Socks, Hand Mittens – 1 of each

☐ Diapers, diaper cream, wipes – usually the hospital will supply these, so they are optional to pack.

Hospital Essentials for You

- ☐ Change of clothing, pyjamas, slippers, robe, going home clothes, sleep eye mask (for a snooze during labour)

- ☐ Personal Hygiene Items – shampoo, brush, toothbrush, toothpaste, sanitary pads, body soap, makeup (for all those up-close pictures!), lip balm and hand lotion (**lips and hands can get dry during labour**). Taking a shower after delivery will make you feel refreshed – take one as soon as it is safe to do so.

- ☐ Nursing pillow, nursing pads, breast pump, Lanolin

- ☐ Pillow and blanket – the hospital does supply however if you want something comfy from home then feel free to bring it with you

☐ Camera, camcorder, phone and all chargers

☐ Snacks for after delivery

Hospital Essentials for Partner/Birth-Partner

☐ Change of clothing, pyjamas

☐ Personal Hygiene items

☐ Pillow and blanket

☐ Phone and charger

☐ Snacks, Book, magazine

Lastly, **do not forget to bring this book to the hospital!** This chapter gave you the Essentials that you need to take care of yourself and your new baby.

Caring for Yourself

All the baby books out there talk about how to take care of your baby. I will also touch on similar topics later in this book. First, I am going to dedicate a chapter to you!

In this chapter, I will discuss the things I wish I would have known ahead of time. I am going to tell it how it is. The *hard truth*, I call it. For me, the mothers that I knew in my family and friend circle never told me the truth of motherhood. Maybe they didn't tell me the truth because they thought it would scare me enough to not even contemplate having children. Yes, that is probably the reason that mothers don't tell young women the truth about becoming a mother. In this book, I hope to not scare you, but **prepare you for what is to come**. And what is to come, will change your life completely. With this guidebook, I will walk you through it and make sure you are standing tall when the storm known as *"the first six weeks"* is over.

The first six weeks is also known as the **postpartum period**. Some institutions are even naming it the "Fourth Trimester". It is a trimester that is mostly ignored. Many people focus more on the pregnancy and delivery, however, that "fourth trimester", or the first six weeks after childbirth, can be the most difficult and challenging.

I am going to divide this chapter into sections that will discuss: perineum care, C-section care, gastrointestinal health, breast care, musculoskeletal health, nutrition and exercise, menstruation, sleep, deep venous thrombosis, headache, mood, partner, family, sex , and birth control.

Some general tips: no driving for 3-4 weeks if you are taking prescription pain medication. Get sleep when the baby sleeps. Taking a shower can really make you feel renewed and ready for the day! Make sure you moisturize your hands (use unscented moisturizer) often because you will be washing your hands a lot after the baby is born. Lastly, taking a walk outside can make you feel good and is healthy for you! Remember, **you need to take care of yourself in order to take care of your baby!**

Perineum Care

The perineum, by definition, is the area that spans from the anus to the external genitalia. It is the area "down there". After vaginally delivering a 5 – 9 lb baby, your perineum may have been stretched, bruised, torn, and maybe cut intentionally (episiotomy). It will be painful, and the doctor likely will send you home with a prescription for pain medication. The most likely pain medications that you will be given are ibuprofen high dose and acetaminophen +/- codeine. Now, you may need these in the beginning. The pain will be at its worst in the first week. Codeine can sometimes make a baby drowsy or hard to feed so beware of this. Also, the codeine can cause constipation for you. So, instead of the acetaminophen with codeine you could try acetaminophen only.

It is important to take a **stool softener, such as docusate, for the first couple days until you have a bowel movement**. You could also take a laxative to get your bowels going.

Another way to help with perineum pain is an **ice pack to the area 10 minutes at a time**. Do not use any creams in the area unless prescribed by your physician. Make sure to **rinse your perineum with lukewarm water** with a spray bottle (aka peri-bottle or squirt bottle) as needed and pat dry or even better air dry. Most hospitals will give you a spray bottle that you can take home. You can use a mild soap with warm water to wash the area if needed. Rinse after every urination and/or bowel movement. Lukewarm water will bring more blood to the area and with that inflammatory cells that will help heal the area. If you can, **let the area air dry during the day and this will promote healing.** Remember, the first couple days will be the worst but *everyday it will get better*. Remember this! **Everyday it will get better!**

Now, another thing that we must speak about is the lochia. Lochia is the vaginal discharge that you may have for up to six weeks after childbirth. It consists of blood, mucous, and uterine tissue. Expect large amounts in the first four days but then it should slow down. Use sanitary pads and change frequently. Do not use tampons during this time as there is a risk of infection with them when used after recent childbirth. If stitches are used, they most likely will be dissolvable and you will not have to do anything about them.

Afterpains are also another thing you will experience. They are uterine cramps that you will feel as your uterus goes back to its original size. Cramps will last for a couple of days and will be more noticeable during breastfeeding. During breastfeeding a hormone is released that helps your uterus shrink to its original size. Because of this, you may also have a gush of lochia while breastfeeding. Remember this is normal. If the afterpains are not tolerable, then take a pain medication as noted above. Walking may also help relieve afterpains.

Before and after childbirth, you can help keep your pelvic floor muscles strong with Kegel exercises. Most women have heard of them but are not sure what they are. Kegel exercises are when you tighten your pelvic floor muscles, hold for 8-10 seconds, then release for 10 seconds and repeat 10 times. You should do these three times a day. Kegel exercises help strengthen the pelvic floor muscles thus decreases your risk for urinary and/or fecal incontinence and uterine/bladder/or rectal prolapse (when the organ falls into the vaginal canal due to weak muscles). The issue of prolapse may come on later in life. Today, this issue of incontinence and prolapse is more recognized and there are pelvic physiotherapists that are trained in even more specific exercises than Kegels.

When to Seek Medical Attention…

- If you are experiencing severe pain in perineum that is not relieved by your pain medications
- If you are experiencing severe abdominal pain
- If you are experiencing foul smelling vaginal discharge
- If you are experiencing burning on urination, increased frequency of urination, blood in the urine, pain on the sides of your back (your flank)
- If you experience a fever (temperature $\geq$ 38°C)
- If you experience a fever (temperature $\geq$ 38°C) especially with any of the following: perineum pain, foul vaginal discharge, severe

abdominal pain, pain on urination, leg pain, headache

- If you are soaking one or more pad per hour, passing clots, and/or passing bright red blood
- If you are having redness, swelling, tenderness, or pain in your legs
- If you are experiencing chest pain, shortness of breath, palpitations, dizziness, blurry vision, headache, nausea, vomiting, rash

C-Section Care

Having a Caesarian section (C-section) is hard on your abdominal wall muscles. So, the first rule is **no heavy lifting over 10 lbs for up to 6 weeks after having a C-section**. No strenuous exercise for 6 weeks. Walking in moderation is safe and healthy.

Regarding the incision area, keep it clean and let it air dry throughout the day. If your doctor has given any creams or antibiotics, then use them as prescribed.

Before you leave the hospital, make sure you ask if the stitches are dissolvable or not. If they are not, then you will need to make an appointment to have them removed in 5 days (this may vary, so follow your doctor's instructions). If you have closure strips (or also known as steri-strips) applied onto of the wound, these will fall off on their own. If they do not, then after 7 days they can be removed. Once your stitches or steri-strips are removed, you can begin to slowly massage the incision area. This will help with healing and promote blood flow to the area. Once the area is healed, if you wish, you can help reduce the scar by applying Bio-oil or a silicone gel.

Pain after a C-section is common and you can take the prescription pain medicine as prescribed. Also, you will still have lochia even after a C-section, as discussed under *Perineum Care*.

When to Seek Medical Attention…

- If you have any of the following at your incision site: redness, swelling, drainage, foul odour, opening of the wound, or increasing pain
- If you have any of the signs mentioned above with fever
- If you experience severe abdominal pain with or without fever

Gastrointestinal Health

Bringing a child into the world is hard work and your body tells you this in the weeks after birth. Constipation is an issue every new mom will face. The gut is slowed down due to the natural process of labour and delivery. In addition, if you received any pain medication then these also contribute to the slowing of the digestive system. Most women will have a bowel movement by day three after birth. **Tips to help things move along:**

drink plenty of water, try prune juice 1 cup a day and increase as tolerated, and a high fibre diet. If these do not work, then you move on to the stool softeners, such as docusate. Remember, I do recommend taking a stool softener beginning right after birth and take it at least until you have your first bowel movement. If docusate does not work, you can move on to laxatives if needed. Another thing that may help is putting your feet on a step stool while you are trying to have a bowel movement. This will relieve some of the pressure from the perineum. If you are having trouble passing a hard bowel movement, it has been shown that perineal pressure can help. This is where you place the pads of two fingers on the perineum (again, area between vagina and anus) and apply pressure. This may facilitate passing of a hard stool.

The big worry about having constipation is hemorrhoids! They are very common after childbirth because of the pressure from the pregnancy and the pushing during delivery. In addition, if you have constipation, then this also contributes to the formation of hemorrhoids. Hemorrhoids are swollen veins near the anus. People can have internal or external hemorrhoids or sometimes both. The external ones are visible, and people can feel a "bump" near their anus. The worry with hemorrhoids is sometimes they can cause bleeding where you would see bright red blood on the toilet paper or drops into the toilet bowl. Even one drop of blood can make the entire toilet bowl look red. Hemorrhoids can cause severe pain if the vein in the hemorrhoid becomes clotted or thrombosed or ulcerated. Then, you may need a procedure, usually done in the emergency room, to cut open the hemorrhoid. Other complications from hemorrhoids include infection and pruritus or itchiness.

How can we treat hemorrhoids? Well, there is over-the-counter Preparation H, which contains phenylephrine. Phenylephrine is a vasoconstrictor, so it makes the blood vessels or veins in the hemorrhoid smaller. These products are meant to be inserted into the anus using the applicator that comes with it. Witch Hazel, a liquid astringent, also can help relieve itch and pain when applied (you can use a cotton ball to apply to area). There are also prescription creams such as Anusol HC and Proctofoam HC which contain hydrocortisone. Hydrocortisone is a steroid that will decrease the inflammation in the blood vessels and relieve the itch. They also contain pramoxine that helps to relive itch.

Another remedy for hemorrhoids includes a sitz bath, where you sit in the bath with lukewarm water for 15-20 minutes up to three times a day. You can add a teaspoon of Epsom salt if you wish. At most health stores they sell a plastic sitz bath that can be placed over the toilet so you can sit in it. It mainly helps with the pain associated with hemorrhoids.

You can take your prescription pain medication also as needed. A donut pillow can give you hemorrhoid pain relief when sitting. It can be purchased at most pharmacies or health stores. Again, not everyone will get hemorrhoids but please be aware of the things that you can do to relieve the pain and discomfort associated with them.

When to Seek Medical Attention…

- You have gone 5 days without a bowel movement
- You have hemorrhoids that do not improve with the creams applied
- You have hemorrhoids that are causing severe pain
- You are having bright red blood from the rectum

Breast Health

I have a term that I used for a while after having my first child: **Triangle of Pain**. The points of the triangle of pain are the two breasts and the vaginal area. It was always a laugh between my partner and I whenever I used my hands to outline the triangle of pain. We already talked about one point of the triangle, the perineum, now, let us discuss the breasts. The two other points of the triangle.

During your pregnancy, your breasts will increase in size by about two cup sizes. You may develop stretchmarks on your breasts from this increase in size. Your nipple area, aka "areola" will darken in colour, increase in size, and small bumps will rise around it. Those bumps provide lubrication to the baby while they are sucking. It is advised to not stimulate the breasts during pregnancy as it could cause milk release and possibly stimulate uterine contraction. Oxytocin is a hormone that is involved with milk production and release. Oxytocin stimulates contraction of myoepithelial cells, causing milk to be ejected into the ducts in the breast tissue. Oxytocin release also causes contraction of the uterine smooth muscle. This helps to bring the uterus back to its normal size. While breastfeeding, you will feel period-like cramps and you may feel a gush of vaginal discharge. Some women experience a negative mood effect during breastfeeding. This is because some women have an increased stress response to oxytocin. For them, it can cause increased anxiety, irritability, and depressed mood while the baby is breastfeeding. If this happens to you, be aware that it could be from the oxytocin hormone and nothing that you are doing wrong. You should notify your physician if you are having these symptoms.

If you plan on breastfeeding

After your baby is born, the baby will be placed immediately on your breast for feeding. Even though you have very little milk, which at this point is called colostrum, this sucking effect by the newborn is required to stimulate milk production. Remember, the stomach of a newborn is about the size of a cherry, so they do not need much milk to feel full. Many new moms feel guilty that they do not have a lot of milk in the beginning. However, the baby does not need much in those first couple days. Sometimes, formula supplementation is necessary in those first few days. We will talk about formula supplementation in the *Feeding* Chapter. Colostrum is a fluid that is rich in vitamins, minerals, immunoglobulins (these protect the baby from infection), fat, protein, and sugar. If you receive a vaccination during pregnancy, the immunoglobulins you produce will be transferred to your baby. Speak to your doctor about any vaccination updates you may need.

The **more often you feed your baby, the more your breasts will be stimulated to produce milk**. So, put your newborn on the breast! Between day two to five after birth, your breasts will begin to produce milk. For some women it can take up to seven days. Many women experience engorgement at this point. And it is exactly what it sounds like. Your breasts are engorged! Engorged with milk! Your breasts will feel hot, heavy, hard, and swollen. Don't worry, this feeling will go away in a couple days.

Here are some things you can do to help with the uncomfortable feeling of engorgement and some things you should avoid:

- Taking hot showers will help with pain and will help release milk to decrease engorgement

- Cabbage leaves can be placed in the fridge and then applied onto the breasts. They help draw out excess fluid from the breast.

- Apply ice packs to the breasts maximum 10 minutes at a time

- Do not use tea bags on the nipples, this has been shown to dry up the nipples which will cause more pain

- Do not clean your nipples with water and soap – this again will dry them. You can rinse them gently with lukewarm water.

- Lanolin is a moisturizer made from sheep wool and can be applied to the nipple to help prevent cracking or dryness of the nipple.

Some women get skin irritation or allergy from lanolin and get a red rash around the nipple area. If this happens, discontinue use and you can use Vaseline on the nipple but wipe off before the next feeding.

- You can manually/hand express some milk by massaging your breast from the outer edges toward the nipple or use your breast pump to release a small amount of milk to ease the pain

Other things that women may use to help with nipple pain are nipple shells. You place them over each nipple and you can wear your bra over them. They are plastic shells that work by not letting your nipple come in direct contact with your nursing pad or bra. It also gives some breathing room for your nipples. Wearing a supportive bra/nursing bra can help also. Nursing pads work to absorb any milk leaking from your breasts. There are different brands and it is best to experiment and find which one you like more. **Remember to change**

nursing pads frequently as the increase in moisture can cause infection, including fungal infection of the nipple. This fungus can then be transferred to the newborn and they can develop thrush. Thrush is an oral fungal infection and it causes white spots on the baby's tongue or sides of mouth. If you see this, take your baby to the doctor. Give your nipples lots of air time so they can air dry.

During the first six weeks and perhaps afterwards, you will find your breastmilk will leak. Triggers include: manipulation of the breast, thinking about breastfeeding, hearing a crying baby, seeing a baby breastfeeding, and basically anything having to do with a baby.

Prescription medicines may also help with breast pain. Just remember any prescription medicine that you take has potential to enter the breastmilk so ask your doctor about it. Ibuprofen and acetaminophen are safe to take if engorgement becomes very painful. There are also prescription creams for nipple pain – so please ask your physician.

If you do not plan on breastfeeding

Some women make the decision not to breastfeed. Either it is their personal choice, or they cannot breastfeed due to a medical condition or medications that they take. So, what happens after the baby is born? You should not put the baby to the breast. Any sucking on the breast will stimulate your breasts to produce milk. Wear a supportive bra for comfort and you can use ice packs to the breast held for 10 minutes at a time for pain. Once your body realizes that the baby has not been on the breast, your breasts will change and become softer. If you have too much pain you could pump the breast just to release enough milk, 10-20 mL, for pain relief.

When to Seek Medical Attention…

- If your breasts are very painful, red, and you have a fever, this may mean you have an infection
- If you are having trouble breastfeeding – as this may give you breast pain and may affect the amount of milk your baby is receiving
- If you are having nipple pain – this may indicate nipple infection
- If you have pain on breastfeeding – as this could be sign of infection or trouble with feeding technique

Musculoskeletal Health

Many **new mothers develop back pain, neck pain, and wrist pain**. Back pain and neck pain can happen from improper posture. When you are breastfeeding you should use the nursing pillow or as many pillows as you need to **bring the baby's body close to your breast**. If you do not bring the baby close to the breast, then you will end up bending forward and bending your neck forward so that you can bring your breast closer to the baby. So, instead, I want you to bring the *baby* closer to the breast.

Another musculoskeletal concern is wrist pain. Wrist pain is also a common complaint as new mothers hold their baby's head by placing their thumb on one side of the head and their fingers on the other side. Many new mothers will use this hold to bring the baby's head closer to the nipple when breastfeeding. After the baby has latched, then the new mother's wrist is flexed, and ongoing flexion will cause inflammation of the tendons of the wrist. With time, the new mother may develop wrist tendonitis and/or carpal tunnel syndrome. Carpal tunnel syndrome is an inflammation of the tendons of the carpal tunnel in the wrist which then causes compression of the nerve. This, in turn, can cause you to experience numbness, tingling, or even weakness of the hands. Tendonitis is inflammation of the tendons and this can cause pain. Solutions to these musculoskeletal pains include prevention as described above, acetaminophen or ibuprofen as needed, good back support during breastfeeding, back brace, and/or wrist braces, massage therapy, and physiotherapy. You should always try to bring baby closer to your breast rather than try to bring your body towards the baby.

If after one month of giving birth you still have pain in the back, hips, or pelvis then speak to your doctor. Childbirth is a traumatic experience on the body and some women do get fractures, misalignment, and/or sprains/strains of the muscles or tendons. Your doctor may order some testing for you such as x-rays, an ultrasound, and/or a bone scan.

Nutrition & Exercise

Now, let's talk about what you should be eating now that your pregnancy is over. You should continue to take your prenatal vitamin daily while breastfeeding. This will ensure that you and your baby get the essential nutrients required. Vitamin D, 1000 IU (international units) once daily is also recommended. Remember to take your prenatal on a full stomach. Taken on an empty stomach it can cause nausea and stomach upset. Alright, so what about calories? During pregnancy, it is recommended to take an extra 500 calories a day, equivalent to one piece of toast with peanut butter. While breastfeeding, you can continue with this recommended calorie intake. In terms of diet and what foods to eat, keep it well rounded. A good mix of fruits, vegetables and meats. Health Canada recommends half the plate with vegetables/fruits, 1/4 with meat and 1/4 with grains/carbohydrates. Red meat and green vegetables will give you an extra boost of iron. Some women are anemic or have low iron during pregnancy. Your doctor may recommend an iron supplement.

Hydration is key after childbirth. Water, water, water! **To have good milk production you need to stay hydrated**! You will hear old wives' tales of "you need to drink milk to make milk" and I will tell you when the elder women of the family insist on it, it is hard to say no. I fell for this myth after I had my first baby and then I switched to water. Signs of dehydration: weakness, dizziness, headache, headache while breastfeeding, low milk supply, dry and/or cracked lips, dry mouth, dry hands, and decreased urine output. I would always keep multiple water glasses/bottles in the area where I was breastfeeding. Whenever you breastfeed you will feel an intense thirst. This is your body's feedback to make sure you take more fluids to replace the fluid you are losing while the baby is drinking. Respond to that intense thirst feeling and drink fluids!

Now, what about exercise? After having a baby, it is not recommended to do any type of vigorous exercise for up to 6 weeks. Things like walking and light exercise are recommended. Ladies, you will feel fatigued and exhausted with a newborn. This is a given. However, a **short walk in nature can give you the boost in energy** that you may require and were hoping for. Being outside is always good for the baby too! Once the first six weeks are over, you may wish to start an exercise program to get your body back in shape. The only warning I will give you is if you are still breastfeeding, then you need to time your workout appropriately. Exercise burns calories and releases toxins and radicals in fat and muscle. This occurs more with high intensity exercise. These biological compounds can sometimes make breastmilk taste different. So, breastfeed your baby and then start that workout! After exercising, there will be sweat on your skin and breasts. Some babies do not like that salty taste. So, if they seem irritable when you breastfeed after exercise, then just rinse off the breast with water before breastfeeding. In addition to this, make sure you wear a supportive bra to prevent breast pain after exercise. Remember to continue to eat healthy, take an extra 500 calories a day, and continue your prenatal vitamins and vitamin D.

Menstruation

A common question I get from patients that I see for postpartum visits is "When should I expect to get my period again?" I always tell women that it can be variable. Some women get it in the first month after giving birth. Some women don't get it for one year. **Most women get their period 6-8 weeks after birth.** Due to hormones that are controlled and released during breastfeeding, menstruation can be inhibited. Can you still ovulate without having a period? The answer is Yes! Even if you are not having your period, there is a possibility of getting pregnant. We will talk about birth control later in this Chapter.

Sleep

Oh, sleep... What is that again? Yes, this is what you will be saying once that baby comes. And ladies, this is the cold, hard truth. You know, I never had any warning about this. "Oh yes, it will be fine", "You get used to it",

"Your body is built for this"... Yes, they said these phrases but the truth, the truth never came out. Let me tell you the truth. Once that baby comes, say goodbye to your restful, eight-hour nights of dreamy sleep. This is the truth. Babies are not programmed to sleep through the night. The number one reason is because they get hungry! Usually, **babies will wake up every 2-3 hours to drink**. This is all day and all night. The only solid advice I can give you for those first six weeks is this: **try to get at least one three-hour stretch of sleep in a 24-hour period.** This will allow you to get into deep sleep and allow you to feel refreshed. So, do what you must do to try to get a three-hour stretch. Remember my advice is to sleep when your baby sleeps! You could also get family or close friends to hold the baby so that you can sleep. Pump your breastmilk if you must and leave a bottle ready. If you are formula feeding this can be easier done because you and your partner can divide the responsibility of the feedings.

Deep Venous Thrombosis (DVT)

DVT is a condition where a blood clot forms in the deep veins of the legs. It has higher incidence in pregnancy and the postpartum period due to the nature of hormone levels in the blood. How will you know if you have it? You will feel pain in your calf and/or it will appear red and swollen. You may also have fever. Sometimes the DVT can move and travel up to the lungs. This is called a pulmonary embolus (PE). If you have a blood clot, there is medication to prevent further blood clots. What you can do to prevent a DVT is walk! After you give birth, do not stay lying down for long. **Make sure you start walking** around your home or take short walks outside. Even if you had a C-section, make sure you stay mobile! Also, make sure you stay hydrated!

When to Seek Medical Attention…

- You have pain, redness, fever, and/or swelling in your calf
- If you experience shortness of breath and/or chest pain, cough, coughing up blood - this may indicate a pulmonary embolism

Headache

Headaches are a very common complaint after giving birth and can be due to multiple reasons. **Breastfeeding headache** is caused by oxytocin hormone release when breastfeeding starts. Oxytocin stimulates the milk let-down, or release, and this quick release can bring on a headache. This usually goes away within two weeks. You will get an intense thirst feeling while the baby breastfeeds if you are dehydrated. This **dehydration also contributes to headache.** When the baby drinks, you drink water too!

Tension headache is something I also experienced. Think of tension headache as a way your body releases the "tension" or stress that you are feeling. Feeling tense or stressed contracts our muscles without us knowing it and this can bring on pain. This includes contraction of scalp and facial muscles. My headache would come at the base of my skull and more on the right side. I still feel this headache come on if I am in a stressful situation. What can you use to help relieve your headache? Acetaminophen and ibuprofen can help. Take as directed. Sometimes the headache is too painful, and your doctor will prescribe stronger painkillers. Just be wary of these medications going into the breastmilk if you are breastfeeding. Other things that can help include: massage, heat packs, anything you can do to relax, and stay hydrated with water.

When to Seek Medical Attention...

- Headache that does not get better with acetaminophen and/or ibuprofen

- Headache that increases in severity or limits your function
- Headache associated with one or more of the following: fever, dizziness, changes in vision, numbness and/or tingling in the body, changes in speech, vomiting, nausea, weakness in the extremities, worse on standing/sitting up

Mood

Under this section I want to talk about the Lioness instinct, postpartum blues, and depression.

The **Lioness instinct is a term that I use to describe new mothers**. Why, you would ask? The mother Lioness will do anything to protect her child. New mothers have this instinct. **You will not be weakened by the physical and mental demands of being a new mother**. Women, the Lioness instinct is normal! It is survival. As parents, we are genetically programmed to take care of our young in order to ensure their survival. Take the time to discuss these feelings with close family or friends. New mothers want to spend time with the new baby for bonding and to protect it. This is normal, so do not feel guilty when others say "you never let me hold the baby" or "you never let me dress the baby". You are the mother and the first weeks are important for bonding. This feeling does ease with time, but I want to let you know that you may experience this feeling.

Having a new tiny, sweet newborn is very exciting. You expect to be full of joy and love. The fact is that most mothers will experience the "baby blues" or **postpartum blues**. They begin within the first three to five days after birth. Couple the hormonal changes after giving birth, the stress of having a newborn, and no sleep, then you have a mixture that can easily lead to mood problems. Mood is dependent on chemical concentrations in the brain and any changes can affect the way we feel.

With postpartum blues, women may experience mood swings, crying, impatience, irritability, restlessness, anxiety, fatigue, insomnia, and poor concentration. These symptoms should be gone by two weeks after birth. **If the symptoms of postpartum blues do not go away in two weeks, then the blues might be turning into postpartum depression.**

Let's go back and talk about how you can deal with the blues. Talk, talk, talk. Have someone to talk to. A spouse, a friend, a parent or a sibling. If it gets very difficult to manage, then consider seeking medical attention. Counselling can be helpful if you do not have someone to talk to. Most hospitals or mental health associations have anonymous 24/7 hotlines. Let your feelings out, this truly is the best way. Use a journal for writing your feelings down. Other things to help with the blues include: maintaining a healthy diet, staying hydrated, taking your prenatal vitamins, taking a walk outside in nature, doing something relaxing or that you enjoy, going out of the house on your own to your favourite store or for a coffee, and attending a new mom support group.

My sister would always say to me "you will have a big cry-out around day three. Just let yourself cry it out" and I tell you, it helped! I am lucky that my blues went away on their own. With my first child, I experienced the baby blues. For the first week it was the worst. I felt inadequate, I felt exhausted, I felt sad and it was all confusing. Why did I feel this way? I just had a baby! I have been waiting all this time to meet her and now I can't stop crying? It was a very frustrating time. What I did to help was talk with my partner about how I was feeling. I talked with my sister who had a baby already. I had a pamphlet from the local health unit about a new mother's emotions and I would read it frequently. I would sit on the porch and enjoy the nature to try to calm myself.

Postpartum depression occurs when the "baby blues" last more than two weeks. It can occur within 3 weeks of delivery and can last over a year after the birth. It is due to an imbalance of brain chemicals. Women experience the following: sad mood, decreased energy, decreased concentration, insomnia or hypersomnolence (increased need for sleep), loss in interest in usual activities/hobbies, feelings of guilt, decreased appetite, general overall feeling of being "slowed down", and most importantly these symptoms can lead to suicidal or homicidal thoughts. This sounds scary. I know. Therefore, it is so important to know the signs of postpartum depression so that if you are developing this, then you can seek medical attention. The doctor may suggest prescription medication and/or counselling. Sometimes postpartum depression runs in families, so it is good to ask your mother if she had this after her births.

Some women are taking prescription medication for anxiety and/or depression before the pregnancy. **This should be continued during pregnancy and after the birth of the baby**. Prescription medicine can help keep mood and anxiety stable and most of them are safe during pregnancy and breastfeeding. Speak to your doctor to make sure that the one you are taking is safe. Some women who stop their medicine because they are worried about how it would affect the pregnancy or child, experience postpartum depression at a much higher rate then the general population. Anxiety, depression, and stress in the pregnant woman can be transferred to the baby in-utero. If the pregnant mother is feeling stressed, then the baby senses that the outside environment is a stressful and dangerous place. There is ongoing research about this. Research is showing that a mother's stress changes the baby's brain chemicals and may predispose them to anxiety, ADHD (attention deficient hyperactivity disorder), and depression later in life. Do your best while pregnant to be less stressed. If you feel anxious or depressed, please see a doctor to discuss it.

Sometimes women also experience postpartum anxiety or obsessive-compulsive disorder (unwanted thoughts or impulses). There have been reported cases of postpartum psychosis where new mothers may have paranoia, hallucinations, and strange behaviours. Make sure you seek help and go to the closest emergency room to see a doctor. The most important thing is to remember that if **you have any of the symptoms described, then ask for help! If you have postpartum blues, depression, or other mental health concerns, remember, it does not make you weak! You are strong because you can identify it and seek treatment.**

When to Seek Medical Attention...

- If you experience any combination of the following, especially for more than two weeks: sad mood, decreased energy, decreased concentration, insomnia or hypersomnolence, loss in interest in usual activities/hobbies, feelings of guilt, decreased appetite, general overall feeling of being "slowed down", suicidal or homicidal thoughts, high anxiety

- Seek immediate attention if you have thoughts of harming yourself or baby or anyone else or are having paranoia or hallucinations

Partner

I want to remind you of someone who is easily forgotten during this hectic time - your partner! With you so busy trying to recover from childbirth and taking care of a newborn, it is easy to put your partner on the sidelines. When a baby is born, the mother can usually easily go into "mother mode" and take over all the responsibilities. We need to remember, that our partner can be of great help! **Remember to include your partner in baby activities.** Your partner needs time to connect with the newborn too! **By getting your partner involved, it can establish a lifelong relationship of shared care of the children.** Ask your partner to help with feedings, diaper changes, bath time, holding the baby, sleep time, and more. I believe in getting your partner involved as early as day one. This way they get comfortable with caring for the baby. Your partner may need direction in duties so feel free to tell them what you would like them to do. This could be anything from picking up sanitary pads from the store to rocking the baby to sleep so you can get some early shut eye. Make your partner feel important by giving them time with the newborn and having them actively participate in parenting.

Your partner can be a great help once the baby is born. They can also be a great source of support. As a new mother, you will have lots of emotions. Talk about your emotions and feelings to your partner. Tell them what is on your mind. My husband is such an excellent partner in life and a terrific father to our children. I got him involved in the childcare from day one. He was nervous to change diapers and clothing, just like I was, but with practice we both became experts. With words of encouragement and by telling him how it helps with bonding, he was eager to help. He never hesitates when something needs to be done for the children. We work as a team when it comes to taking care of our children. I encourage you to get your partner involved in the childcare early on and you will both benefit as the years go on.

Talk to your partner about how you are feeling. Ask them for support and for help with the baby. **Communication is key in any relationship**. Ask them how they are feeling too! You don't want to neglect your partner during this exciting time. Don't forget that you are a couple and still need to be friends with each other and show each other how you care for each other.

Family

With your newborn in your arms and partner by your side, you will feel like a family. It is a wonderful and heartwarming feeling. In this section however, I want to talk about the extended family - the parents, siblings, and in-laws. Family can be supportive and useful, but they can also be critical at times.

Let's start with the positive points. Family can be supportive. Your mother and mother-in-law will likely offer their delivery and postpartum tales. They will help you with anything you need for the baby. I would always make sure to use my family if they were over to visit. I would either sleep while they held the baby, do some chores, or take a shower. Don't be afraid to ask! They want to help you very much and will most likely jump to complete any task you give them. This was my experience.

Sometimes family may overextend their welcome and then disrupt your newborn's sleep or your own sleep schedule. Everyone has an opinion about everything, especially child-rearing. My own sister warned me about this before I had my first baby. She said that everyone will have an opinion and all you have to say is "Oh, I didn't think about it like that, I might use that next time, thank you". So, the person giving the advice is satisfied and the one receiving it can put it in their back pocket. What I am saying is that you should not let any statements get to you. Just acknowledge it and move on. **You are the child's mother and *you know what is best for the baby*.**

Sex & Birth Control

A common question from women during postpartum visits is "When can we have sex?". From patient anecdotes and medical textbooks, it sounds like six weeks is a minimum wait time. **You need time for the perineum to heal and it is generally healed at six weeks**. How do you know that it is healed and is ready for intercourse? Well, you know when you attempt intercourse and you are pain-free. If it is painful at all, then stop, and retry in one week.

Will sex be different after you have a child? Well, the actual physical act and mechanics are the same. As a couple, you both have to put in more of an effort to have sex. What do I mean by this? Now with a small baby it may be harder to maintain the same frequency of sex as you had previously. If it is a priority, then you need to make time for it. Talk with your partner about it and discuss ways to make it work. The key in any relationship is communication. I say it again, talk with your partner about expectations and goals for sex. Sexual health is important, so don't disregard it.

Another important topic is birth control. One myth I want to clear right away is that "when you breastfeed you can't get pregnant". This is not true. I have met many women that have become pregnant when they were breastfeeding. If you go back to the studies revolving this, the only way that breastfeeding acts as contraception is if the woman breastfeeds exactly every three hours in 24 hours. This does not even guarantee that ovulation won't take place. So, do not depend on breastfeeding for birth control. The combined oral contraceptive pill (OCP) may decrease milk supply if you are breastfeeding. There is a progesterone only pill that can be used for contraception if breastfeeding. Other options include intrauterine device (IUD), patch, injection, ring, condoms, and permanent sterilization (tubal ligation or vasectomy). Remember to talk with your doctor about all the options available to you.

I am going to end this chapter with a statement that I said in the beginning. *You need to take care of yourself in order to take care of your baby! Remember, everyday it will get better!* I hope this chapter has given you all the information you need to take care of yourself in the postpartum period.

How Life Will Change

Having a baby is a big decision and certainly a big life decision. Your life truly changes after a baby comes into the picture. In this chapter we will discuss how your emotions and priorities change, how your free time and roles change, and how the romance with your partner changes. Let's begin!

Emotions

You will love your baby with your heart and soul! Instant attachment and an instant feeling of needing to protect the baby. Both you and your partner will be consumed with this new little life in your hands! Unfortunately, becoming a parent will allow for the emotional pendulum to swing back and forth quite readily. You now have this little baby in your hands and YOU ARE responsible for this little human. You need to take care of it so it can grow. You need to feed it. You need to keep it warm. You need to teach this baby so that it can grow up in the world and be an independent adult one day. You already start to worry about your newborn. Why is the baby crying? Is that poop normal? What is that red spot on its bum? Did I swaddle the baby right? **Panic and worry are normal! I repeat, panic and worry are normal! That means YOU ARE A PARENT!** Let's just put it this way, it is part of the job description.

As a new parent, there are a million questions and concerns going through your head. Ok. Stop right there. Close your eyes. Take a deep breath. Now, imagine your little new baby. Just focus on providing the best care to that little baby and giving it lots of love. The newborn period is as hectic as you make it seem. Your mindset is important too. Be positive and accomplish those small tasks as they come. The baby can feel when you are stressed and in turn will feel stressed also. A stressful baby will indeed make your day longer and more difficult. Practice ways to de-stress and try to remain positive. As the days go by, it will get better! The baby will grow out of the newborn period and you both will find a peaceful rhythm that will flow.

Priorities

You will find that after the baby is born, the **baby is priority #1** and you will find that every decision – either major or minor life decision – will have the baby as a main factor to consider when making the decision. For example, many new fathers tell me that they find themselves driving slower and with more caution because they want to be safer, even when the baby is not in the car. There is no way around this, the baby is a MAJOR part of your life now and with every decision you will have to consider "where does my baby fit in with this". You are a family now and families make decisions together.

Free Time

Another major change in your life will be amount of free time you have. When you were single, all your time was for you. Whatever you felt like doing is what you did. Then, you were in a relationship, now your time was shared with your partner. So, you think you had no free time before the baby is born. Well, when the baby comes your free time decreases considerably. As you become a more experienced parent, you will learn how to manage your time and eventually, I mean years down the road, your free time will increase. This also coincides with the child growing older. Your child will then be preoccupied with his/her own play and work.

When can you sneak in free time? When the baby naps, it is a great time to finish up any work you have pending, such as laundry or washing the dishes. **Mommy time is important**. When you feel refreshed, you will have more energy to take care of the baby. Mommy time can fit well in early morning hours, during baby naptime, and after bedtime. If you need sleep, then sleep when baby sleeps. Mommy time is reserved for baths, showers, having a relaxing cup of coffee, reading a novel, or watching your favourite show. I have said this before and I will say it again, a short walk outside is great mommy time too. Some quiet time for you. Please do not lose yourself after you have a child. Being a mother can be very hectic at times, but you must *remember who you are as a person*. Mommy time helps keep you grounded. Other things that you may need to fit in your free time are: couple time and visiting family and friends. **Making a daily to-do list in the morning** can help you complete small tasks during the day and help you work towards any goals you have made for yourself.

Roles

Becoming a mother is a new role for you. It will be a role you add onto your list of roles you already have. The key to being a person with multiple roles is *balance*. **You need to have balance so that you do not resent**

any of your roles. For myself, I am a Mother, Wife, Daughter, Big Sister, Doctor, Teacher, and Writer. These roles require time commitment and dedication. Be confident that you can take on your roles. If you feel like you need help balancing your roles, talk to your partner, family and/or friends for advice.

I will tell you that learning how to balance all your roles will be a lifelong, ongoing process. For me, sometimes my career took more of my time. Sometimes I would take a one week "staycation" just to stay at home with the kids. Other days, I would have a date night planned after a long day at work and the babysitter would put the kids to sleep. I would see them for a short time that night. I have learned that it is difficult to achieve balance if you neglect one of your roles more than the others. When I spend more time on work and writing then I feel inadequate as a wife and mother. When I spend time with the kids, sometimes I think about how much work is waiting for me at the office and what rough draft number my next book is in.

Learning how to balance my roles has been a great lesson to me. Once your baby comes, you will also learn how to balance. Just remember, if things begin to feel stressful and you are unable to maintain your roles – then talk about it with someone close to you and discover what is best for you, your health, and your family.

Romance

Having a newborn at home makes it very difficult to find times for romance. Romance does not mean only sex. Sex is important to keep your relationship thriving. My advice is to have an open conversation with your partner about expectations. Remember, as parents it may feel like "work" now to have sex because you add in fatigue and crying children, then the desire and energy to have sex decrease. Find what works for you and your partner. Romance can include other things, such as, handholding, kissing, compliments, and/or hugging. Try to do these things daily with your partner. You must keep the romance alive!

After the arrival of your newborn, you will eventually get into a new balance and rhythm. It is all worth it for your new, precious little baby.

Feeding

In this chapter, I am going to talk about feeding your baby. We will talk about breastfeeding, formula feeding, and everything you need to know.

Breastfeeding

Benefits of Breastfeeding

I am sure you have heard these phrases before: *"Breastfeeding is natural", "It will come naturally", "Your body is made for it".* Let me tell you that my experience with breastfeeding was not like they always talk about in the books. Breastfeeding is something a woman's body is capable of. Let's put it in scientific terms. A female body has two mammary glands that can produce a nutrient-rich fluid that offspring can ingest in order to survive. "Whoa! Dr. Doko that sounds amazing!" you say. Yes! It is amazing. It is remarkable how the human body can provide this food for the baby. There are many benefits to breastfeeding. Breastmilk contains hundreds of healthy compounds including immunoglobulins that protect the baby from infection. Immunoglobulins are the antibodies that the mother has - so any vaccinations that you get during pregnancy will give extra protection to the baby too! Talk to your doctor and see what vaccines you are eligible for. There are additional health benefits for the baby if they breastfeed, including decreased rates of obesity, diabetes, and cancer. Breastfed babies also have fewer infections and allergies.

Breastfeeding benefits the mother also. It can reduce the mother's risk of breast and ovarian cancer, it is less costly than formula, it is easier to do than prepare formula, and it helps to bring the uterus back to normal size quicker. Breastfeeding is very convenient also - you can feed your baby anywhere and anytime. In addition to all those benefits, breastfeeding helps you lose that baby weight! It burns up to 600 calories a day. Both baby and mother benefit from the bonding experience that breastfeeding provides. The closeness that is required allows the baby to feel safe and the mother to bond with the baby. If you or your partner are bottle feeding, just remember to keep the baby close to your body to promote bonding.

You would think that because scientifically our bodies are able to provide this function, that it is easy to do. Well, the hard truth is that it is not. Yes, you always hear those stories of women saying "*I never had any problems breastfeeding, my baby drank like an angel*". Then I say to you, yes but what about those mothers with cracked nipples, breast infections, and babies who don't gain weight because they are not sucking properly to get enough milk? In this chapter, we are going to go over how to breastfeed and issues that may arise. We will talk about pumping, bottle feeding, and formula feeding. Lastly, we will talk about how you will know if your baby is getting enough to drink.

Latching & Troubleshooting

It is common practice now to put the baby onto the breast within 1-2 hours of birth. This is required for newborn comfort, mother-newborn bonding, and to stimulate milk production. Human newborns are genetically programmed to suck on a nipple. How neat is that! It is their mode of survival. It is quite amazing to observe that as soon as your newborn is placed near your nipple it will open its mouth, extend it neck, and try to position itself to get its mouth on your nipple.

The act of the baby placing its lips on the nipple and starting to suck is called the **latch**. Is the baby latched on correctly? Is the latch ok? How is the baby latching? The baby should have their top lip at the top part of the nipple. The bottom lip is under the nipple but also covering a part of the areola, the darkened area around your nipple. In this position, the nipple itself should be sitting at the roof of the baby's mouth. The baby sticks its tongue out, the tongue goes under the nipple, then the baby brings the tongue back in while doing a sucking motion with its facial muscles and on doing this the milk is released from the nipple. The location of the baby's lips and the nipple at the roof of the baby's mouth are the two important points for a good latch.

In order to have a good latch you need the baby to open its mouth wide right before latching. You can do this by bringing your nipple close to the baby's nose. The baby will smell the nipple and sense that food is near and available. The baby usually then opens its mouth wide in anticipation of latching. When the baby opens its mouth, then you can direct their mouth to your nipple. Just remember, the top lip goes at the top of the nipple and the bottom lip goes under the nipple and covering part of the areola. **If the baby can get a good latch, it doesn't matter what position you breastfeed in**. By position I am talking about the way you hold your baby while breastfeeding. There are the cross-cradle, cradle, football, and lying positions. What I tell my patients is that **you should breastfeed in whatever position is comfortable for you and baby**.

Just a note here about the baby's skin after a feeding. Sometimes, milk can get into the neck folds so make sure that after a feeding you wipe t he neck and keep it dry. You can use a warm towel with mild soap to clean the area. Moisture in your baby's folds can cause fungus and bacteria to grow and it can become quite severe if you allow it. You can place a bib on the baby if they are spitting up frequently or are getting milk onto its neck frequently.

There is another technique that you can use for breastfeeding called **baby-led latching**. This is where you put the newborn skin-to-skin on your chest, with the baby's face facing your chest. Then, you place your hands gently on the baby's body and let them find the breast on their own. I know what you are thinking. How is that possible? The baby can smell your breast and will bob its head and move its body so that it can find the nipple and feed. It is a very fulfilling experience to watch your newborn work and find the breast on its own. It has the instinct to survive and to find its food source.

In the perfect world, you would have the perfect nipple and the baby would have a perfect latch and suck. However, this may not be the case. Sometimes a woman's nipple is not a good shape to allow for a good latch. One thing that may help with the latch is bringing out the nipple by pulling it gently outwards with your fingers. Another product that might help are **nipple shields.** The nipple shield is placed over your nipple while you breastfeed. The baby sucks on the shield and this stimulates your milk to release. Nipple shields are good products if you have cracked nipples or very painful nipples on feeding and you want to give your nipples a break from feeding.

Something else that can cause trouble with latch is if the baby is very hungry. You might find the baby getting frustrated and crying because it is hungry but cannot latch. This can happen if the baby is crying for food, which is a late hunger sign. Then, because the baby is upset it cannot focus to perform the latch.

Newborns can sense a mother's stress. If you are stressed or worried about the baby feeding, then the baby senses this and will have more trouble latching or feeding. Make sure you have everything ready for your breastfeeding session and try to relax before the session.

Another reason for difficulty in latch is if your baby is not fully awake. **Sleepy babies do not latch well** because they are dozing in and out of sleep so cannot focus to perform the latch. Try to undress the baby all the way down to the diaper, stroke its back, stroke the bottoms of its feet, place a cool cloth on its body, anything you can do to wake that baby up! You can also compress your breasts to try to stimulate some milk flow. Then, bring your nipple to the baby's mouth so they can taste the milk. This might get them interested to drink. Remember, if you are on prescription medication that gets into the breastmilk, the baby may be drowsy from that also. Speak to your doctor about any medications you take and effect on breastfeeding.

A fungal infection of the nipple can be transferred to the baby and cause oral thrush. Thrush can give the baby pain on feeding and your baby may not latch well. Speak to your doctor if you suspect this.

Other medical reasons why baby would not latch well include: **anatomical problems, prematurity, and neurological disorders**. A common anatomical reason for difficult latch is tongue tie. **Tongue tie is where the tongue cannot fully extend past the lips**. There is a minor and quick procedure that can be done to fix tongue tie. Other anatomical problems with the lips (such as cleft lip), throat, or oral cavity could make it difficult to breastfeed. Premature babies have come out of the womb early and may not be ready to perform the latch or have the muscular strength to do. For a baby to suck, there are multiple muscles involved. These include the tongue, throat muscles, facial muscles, and neck muscles. Therefore, many premature babies are bottle fed or tube fed. Taking milk from a bottle involves less muscular effort and no performance of the latch, so it is easier for the baby. Neurological disorders in a newborn may also cause problems with performing the latch and may cause decreased muscular strength and thus a poor sucking reflex.

If you are having trouble breastfeeding, always consult a healthcare professional. Most public health units have supports for new mothers, including breastfeeding clinics or even home visits to help you with breastfeeding. Please, do not feel guilty if you must use those services. Everyone needs help at one point or another.

Feeding Cues

Babies will show feeding cues when they are hungry. They may stick out their tongue or make sucking motions with lips, bring their hands to their mouth and suck on them, turn their head to one side as if looking for the nipple, and start to squirm and seem uncomfortable. Crying is a late hunger sign so try to feed your baby before they start crying for food. Once they start crying for food they will be frustrated and may be harder to feed because they cannot focus to latch. **If you have any doubt if they are hungry or not, just try to offer them a feeding**. If they are hungry, then they will latch. If the baby is not hungry, then it will turn its face away from the breast and will not latch. If the baby is feeding and then is full, the baby will "un-latch" by removing his/her lips from the nipple. Don't underestimate your baby! He/she will let you know when they are hungry or full.

Feeding Cues

- Sticking out tongue
- Making sucking motion with lips
- Bringing hands to mouth
- Turning head to one side looking for nipple

- Getting frustrated
- Crying – this is a late sign

How Often Should You Breastfeed?

How often should you breastfeed? This is a common question among new mothers. Different books try to tell you a certain amount, but I will give you something easier to guide you. If the baby is crying (or starting to become fussy), *put them on the breast*. Feed them! This is called **feeding on demand**. My mother gave me this advice when I had my first child and it saved me lots of crying nights. You may have read that you should breastfeed your baby every 2-3 hours. However, what if the baby is hungry now? The only way to know if your baby is hungry is if you put them on the breast. If they suck, then they are hungry. If they refuse or move their head away, then most likely they are not hungry. I suggest you **use the 2-3-hour mark as a checkpoint**. Most newborn babies will want to drink at least every 2-3 hours. Babies may be hungry more often than every 2 hours and then some may sleep for more than 3 hours. Think of yourself. Are you hungry every 2-3 hours? Perhaps. Maybe you had a large meal 2 hours ago and feel full at the 3-hour mark.

If you are holding them in your arms, they may get upset because they think you are going to feed them. If the baby gets fussy in your arms, try to feed them. Babies can smell the breast. This is a scientific fact. Babies who lie next to their mothers can move their necks and bodies in order to get to the nipple. So, when you are holding them close to your chest, they smell the nipple nearby and may get upset if you do not offer it.

Make sure that you offer the baby a feeding every 2-3 hours minimum. What I recommend for new mothers, especially in the first couple weeks, is to keep track of when you feed your baby. Keep a note of what time you start breastfeeding and this is your start time. For example, you put your baby on the breast at 2 pm. It takes your baby 20 minutes to feed (yes, it is variable how long it takes them to feed, some newborns can take up to an hour in total to feed). Then, the next feed would be at 4-5pm at the latest.

Switching Sides when Breastfeeding

We talked about latch, sucking, positions, troubleshooting for latch and sucking, and when to feed. How long on each breast? **A baby may feed 5-30 minutes on each breast.** Let me explain how you alternate between breasts. Start with one breast, let's call it Side A. So, as an example, the baby latches well, feeds for 15 minutes, then goes off the nipple. Babies will release the latch when they are full or have fallen asleep on the breast. **Once the baby is done one side, always burp the baby**. Any gas can continue to travel through the gut and make the baby uncomfortable. You fed Side A and now either the baby took him/herself off or the baby was sucking intensely and then slowed down and seems to be sucking for comfort (like the baby would do with a pacifier) and may or may not let go of the nipple.

To release the baby manually what you can do is take your pinky finger and put it gently between your nipple and the corner of the baby's mouth. This breaks the latch manually.

Ok, back to the example. You breastfed Side A, 15-minute feed, baby burped, now you should offer the other breast, Side B. Why? Because if the baby is not full then it will take whatever amount it needs to feel full from Side B. The important thing is to offer it. Let's say the baby feeds for 5 minutes on Side B and then you burp the baby. Now, on the next feed, which side do you offer first? The answer is Side B. Why? Because that is the last side the baby fed on. Your **next feeding starts on the side you ended your last feeding**. This is important because that is the breast that will have more milk for the next feeding.

Your breasts produce milk and this can be divided into foremilk and hindmilk. What are the differences? **Foremilk is the milk that comes out of the breast at**

the beginning of a feed. It has a high water content which quenches the baby's thirst. If you ever pump your breast, you will notice this foremilk is whiter in colour. Then comes the hindmilk. The **hindmilk is enriched with high concentration of fat and protein and will keep the baby full for a longer time**. When feeding, remember to offer both sides and start on the last side offered at the previous feeding. Sometimes women use a safety pin that they clip onto the bra side where the last feeding was given. Disclaimer: be careful that the safety pin does not open and may injure the baby or you.

How long does the baby have to feed for? It varies! It depends on the baby's personality also. They may be a fast feeder and be finished both breasts in less than 10 minutes. Or, they may be a slower feeder and take one hour to finish a feed.

Colostrum

In the beginning, your breasts will produce **colostrum**. Colostrum is rich in fat, protein, and immune globulins. Immune globulins are proteins that you have in your blood. They are a part of your immune system. Whenever you received a vaccination or were ill, your immune system made antibodies, also known as immune globulins, to fight the disease or get immunity from a vaccine. These antibodies get passed to the baby and helps them fight off infections. Isn't that remarkable!

In the first 1-3 days of life, the baby will drink the colostrum. Many mothers worry that the newborn is not getting enough milk because of low production. The first 1-3 days is all about the colostrum and the baby's sucking to stimulate your breast to make milk. So, if the baby seems hungry then put the baby on the breast. Let the baby get soothed from the sucking, be close to you (skin to skin) and stimulate your breast tissue to make milk. This way your breasts know that there is a baby to feed.

Babies can be exclusively given breastmilk or formula until they are six months old. You do not have to give your newborn water, tea, juices, or any solid foods. Especially no honey in the first year as it can harbour botulism spores, a bacterium, that can make your baby very sick. **Vitamin D supplementation is also important when you are breastfeeding**. Vitamin D 400 IU (International Units) once a day for the baby is the recommendation. This comes in drops or liquid and both work well.

Supplementing with Formula

Some babies may continue to cry even after a feeding in those first few days. You then try all the soothing techniques we will discuss in the *Crying* Chapter and if none of those work, then consider giving the baby some formula. This is called **supplementing with formula**. I know many guidelines say to use exclusively breastfeeding or exclusively formula but from my experience, this works. When I brought home my first daughter, everything was going great until after one feeding, she wouldn't stop crying. I fed her both sides, tried to soothe her, there was no fever, and it was very frustrating. My mother-in-law was staying with us to help with the new baby and she suggested we try a small amount of formula. So, we gave the baby some formula. She drank 10 mL and fell asleep. We only had to do that maybe two more times before my milk "came in". That is why I suggest having some formula at home, just in case.

Breast Engorgement & Your Milk "Coming In"

Your breasts will make milk on demand. Once the baby empties the breast, the breast will refill with milk, so as the baby drinks more, the more milk your breast will make. On day 3-5, your milk will "come in". Your body will produce lots of milk to make sure there is enough volume for the new baby. When this happens, you will know. Firstly, you will see the milk dripping from the nipple during feeding time. Secondly, you will know because your breasts will be swollen, hard, and painful. We discussed this a bit in the chapter *Caring for Yourself.* What I want to say here is that you should allow the baby to feed on demand. The baby can help you, and you can help the baby. The baby will release your breasts of milk and will relieve your pain. In turn, you provide the baby with nutrients. If you have low milk supply there is a medication that might help, speak to your doctor about it.

Breast engorgement can cause too much volume and sometimes the baby cannot empty the breast fully. Remember, they have small stomachs that require small volumes frequently. During engorgement the **"letdown", or the initial release of the milk,** can be too fast for the baby and they cannot swallow it fast enough. Not every baby has trouble with the fast letdown. Again, I will tell you my experience. My first daughter had this problem with engorgement. The letdown was too fast, and she couldn't tolerate it, so she would take herself off the breast. What I did to help her was I used my manual breast pump to "release" my breast a bit (I would pump 10-20mL) and then put the baby on the breast. This helped and then she would feed!

Other things that will help with engorgement: acetaminophen or ibuprofen, ice packs held for maximum 10 minutes at a time, cabbage leaves on the breasts (not nipples), lanolin cream on the nipple, nipple shells, a hot shower, hand expressing and/or pumping to release the breast so they feel more comfortable (the key here is to not pump all the milk out of the breast, only enough for pain relief, that may be only 10-20 mL), and massaging the breasts. **When massaging the breast, you would focus on any hard spots where the milk ducts may be plugged**. When you massage, expect milk to be released. This will help prevent a blocked milk duct that can be very painful and could even lead to an infection called mastitis.

How your breasts do with engorgement also depends on the feeding personality of the baby. Not all babies are the same. Take my children for example. My first one did not breastfeed well, I would have to undress her to feed, help her with her latch, and she wouldn't empty my breasts well. Even today, she is still a picky eater. Whereas my second daughter, she latched by herself, would empty the breasts, would unlatch herself when she was full, and never required me to give her formula in the first days or for me to pump my breasts to release them for her. And yes, you guessed it, today she is a big eater and never gives me problems. If you are having issues or are finding breastfeeding frustrating, it may not be you, it may be the baby!

Night Feedings

Let's discuss night feedings. The thing you don't want to happen is that you fall asleep while breastfeeding your baby. If the baby is in a position where it cannot breathe well, you risk harming the baby by falling asleep while breastfeeding. Here are some tips to follow so that you can stay awake during night feedings: have a nightlight in the room, have a drink of cold water, sit up while breastfeeding, and/or wash your face with cold water.

Nipple Pain

Another issue I want to mention in this section is **nipple pain**. Prior to having your baby, your nipples will be soft. Then your baby comes and starts to suck at the nipple. **Discomfort is normal when the baby is feeding**. This will go away by end of the first week. Lanolin is a moisturizer for nipples. After every feed gently put some on the nipple only. The nipple is changing from a soft area to something harder so that it is easier to latch onto. If you are having **severe pain, this may also be due to improper latch**, so review how your baby is latching. Severe pain while breastfeeding may also be due to **infection. Make sure you change the nursing pads frequently** as too much moisture at the nipples can cause bacteria or fungus to grow. Let the nipples air dry if you can. If you have continued pain while breastfeeding, make sure to see your doctor.

In the first six weeks, breastfeeding can be difficult as you and baby learn how to get into the rhythm of breastfeeding. You can help by doing a couple things before the breastfeeding session. Babies are very good at picking up on mom's stress level. If the baby feels stressed, then it will have difficulty latching and be difficult to settle. Get everything ready in your breastfeeding area – have your burp cloth ready, your nursing pads, a water bottle, something to read, and anything else you may need. Take some deep breaths.

Get in the mindset of breastfeeding and begin your session.

Above we discussed lots of troubleshooting for different breastfeeding issues. You may or may not encounter these issues. However, I want you to be aware of the problems you can encounter so you know there are solutions available.

Pumping, Bottle Feeding, & Formula Feeding

Pumping

Now, as we talked about above, sometimes you may need to release the milk from your breasts.

Here are some reasons for pumping:
- To help relieve pain in the breasts
- To store milk
- You are away from your baby and need to release your breasts

- You need to release some volume if too much milk is being released at letdown
- You are bottle feeding your baby your breastmilk

Hand expressing is an option. This is where you use both hands and massage the breasts in a motion from the outer edge of the breast and move your hands towards the nipple. This will express milk but may not be enough to get you comfortable. So, having a pump will help in the situations described above.

Should you purchase a manual or electric pump? Manual pumps allow you to control the strength of the suction on the nipple, but it may take longer to pump. Electric pumps can be single or double (both breasts at the same time). The suction effect is stronger, and the upside is it takes less time to pump. Electric pumps can be expensive. I advise you to talk to other new mothers and decide what option is better for you. When I was doing my family medicine postgraduate training interview, I was in the ladies' room and saw one of the other interviewees take out her electric pump. She had a double, top of the line pump. She plugged it in the wall (though they can work on batteries too) and put one suction on each breast and pressed the on button. She did not have to hold the suction in place. I was asking her about it and she told me she had 2-week-old twins at home and had to pump. I felt sympathy for her and proud at the same time. See below for breastmilk storage rules.

Breastmilk Storage Guidelines

- Room temperature: 3-4 hours
- Refrigerator: 3 days
- Thawed milk in refrigerator: 1 day
- Freezer inside the refrigerator: 2 weeks
- Refrigerator freezer (own separate door): 3-6 months
- Deep freezer: 6-12 months

Bottle feeding

Bottle feeding is when you use formula or your own pumped breastmilk and feed it to the baby from a bottle. If you are doing formula feeding exclusively then you will be doing bottle feeding 100% of the time. There are different companies that make baby bottles, and all are good products. Which one is best for your baby? The one that your baby drinks from! You may have to switch bottles if your baby won't drink from the bottle you have chosen. You can bottle feed your pumped breastmilk if you wish. When would you consider bottle feeding? You may consider it if you have severe pain at the nipple when breastfeeding, when you are away from the baby and need someone else to feed the baby, or if you wanted to get some extra sleep and someone else can feed the baby with the bottle. I used to do this sometimes in the night, the baby would feed, go to sleep and I would pump the breast that the baby didn't finish. That would go in the fridge and my husband would bottle feed it to her on the next feeding and this let me get a straight 5-hour sleep that night.

Remember that new bottles need to washed and sterilized. Sterilize the bottles by washing them with warm water and mild dish soap then rinsing and placing in boiling water. Leave them in the boiling water for five minutes then place on drying rack. For the first six months of a baby's life you should sterilize the bottles once a day. Do not wash bottles or components of the bottle in a dishwasher. Dishwasher rinse fluid or washer fluid/pods contain chemicals that may irritate the baby's gut and/or cause allergic reactions and eczema. If you really would like to use the dishwasher then consider purchasing hypoallergenic dishwasher fluid and rinse. Pacifiers should also be sterilized the same way listed above. Stores sell bottle sterilizers that are used in the microwave and you could purchase this if you wish.

Remember to warm up the breastmilk or formula before giving to the baby. It will taste better for them when it is warm. The best way to warm up the milk is to place the bottle in warm water and wait 1-2 minutes. Test the temperature by pouring one drop onto your forearm. Temperature should be lukewarm, like a baby's bath temperature. They do sell bottle warmers and some parents like these because it warms the bottle to the right temperature. Even with bottle warmers, check the temperature of the milk before feeding to the baby. Do not microwave the milk! Microwaving does not heat the milk (or solids for that matter) evenly and causes areas of the milk to be too hot. If you are using thawed breastmilk, taste it first as sometimes due to the freezing and thawing process it develops a bad taste and the baby will not drink it.

Formula Feeding

In this section, I will talk about how much formula the baby needs and the different types of formula. There is ready made formula, which is more expensive than powder formula. Powder formula comes with instructions on how to mix. You can use tap water or bottled water to mix the formula, but you need to boil the water for at least two minutes. Powdered formula is safe in the newborn period if the baby is healthy, full term, and has a healthy immune system. Make sure any formula you purchase is iron-fortified, meaning it has the iron your baby needs.

The main types of formula include milk-based and non-milk-based. **Some newborns have trouble digesting the large cow's milk protein**. These newborns experience the following symptoms: bloating, bloody stools, frothy or watery stools, and crying when having a bowel movement. If your baby has these symptoms make sure you take them to see their doctor. You will likely have to switch to non-milk-based formula. If you are breastfeeding and your newborn has the bowel symptoms listed above, then I recommend you trial a two week no dairy diet as to remove the large cow-milk protein from your breastmilk. If this works, continue with a dairy-free diet until you are done breastfeeding.

All formula products are made to provide all the vitamins, minerals, fat, sugar, and protein that a baby will need. Of course, there are some biochemical compounds and immune proteins that cannot be duplicated. **If you do switch between formulas, then give that product at least one week to see how your baby's bowel movements will change**. If you are using formula you will be able to know exactly how much the baby is getting.

Recommended Intake of Breastmilk or Formula

- For Infants 0-3 weeks old: 8-10 feedings per day, 2-3oz (60-100 mL) each
- For infants 4 weeks to 4 months old: 6-8 feedings daily, 4-5 oz (125-150 mL) each

Make sure you follow the manufacturer's instructions on how to prepare the formula.

How to Know if Your Baby is Getting Enough Milk

In this section, we will talk about how to know if your baby is drinking enough milk. Here are some things to consider: is the baby making enough wet diapers, is the baby having a certain number of bowel movements a day, is the baby growing, and does the baby seem content? **Newborn babies can have up to 8-10 wet diapers a day after day 5 of life**. If your baby is producing less than recommended, then make sure you take them to see a doctor.

See below for the average of wet and soiled (poopy) diapers a day:

- Day 1 of life: at least 1 wet diaper and 1-2 black or dark green soiled diapers
- Day 2: at least 2 wet diapers and 1-2 black or dark green soiled diapers
- Day 3-4: at least 3-4 wet diapers and 3 soiled diapers

- After Day 5: at least 6 wet diapers a day and at least 3 yellow soiled diapers.

Newborns can lose up to 10% of their birthweight in the first week, they then gain it back and start growing. When you take your baby for their check-up at the doctor, they should start to gain weight after the first week of life. They should also be growing in length. Your doctor can plot your baby's growth on a growth chart and monitor it at every visit. Lastly, does your baby seem content or happy? If your baby feeds and then seems content, then most likely the baby is not hungry at the moment.

Growth Spurts

You will get into a nice rhythm with your baby. Then, one day the baby will act as if it is hungry all day long. Your little one will cry even after a feeding as if it is not full. You wonder what is going on. It is a growth spurt! Your baby is drinking more frequently in order to stimulate your breasts to make more volume of milk. The baby will need more volume to support their growth spurt. For formula fed babies, you will find them requiring more formula to be content. During growth spurts babies may want to drink every 1-1.5 hours. **Growth spurts occur at 7-10 days, 2-3 weeks old, 6-8 weeks old, 3 months old, 6 months old, and 9 months old**. Remember, feed on demand during these times to keep the baby fed and content.

Back-to-Back Feedings

Another thing that some babies do is back-to-back feedings before bedtime. You may find that in the evening they seem hungry every 30 minutes to one hour for 2-3 hours before bedtime. This may be confusing because you think "well the baby just drank and shouldn't be hungry right?". Just remember, if the baby is crying, always offer a feeding! Babies that do back-to-back feedings may have a longer sleep after the feedings. Back-to-back feedings are also called cluster feedings.

Gastroesophageal Reflux (GERD)

Let's talk about babies and gastroesophageal reflux or GERD. Some babies spit-up after feedings. This is because their valve that separates the esophagus, the tube that connects the throat with stomach, and the stomach is more relaxed. This can be the case in some babies. If your baby is vomiting, make sure you take them to the doctor. Some babies can have GERD, which is also known as heartburn. The symptoms would be spit-up and the baby seems very uncomfortable if lying flat. Babies that have GERD may arch their back. This is because of the burning pain they feel in their chest from the stomach acid. If your baby displays any of these symptoms, then take them to the doctor.

I hope this chapter has given you clarification on breastfeeding, techniques, and troubleshooting.

When to Seek Medical Attention…

- Baby is not latching properly
- Baby is not feeding the minimum feeds per day
- Baby is not having required wet diapers a day
- Baby is too drowsy/sleepy/limp and may not feed to meet the minimum feedings a day and/or have the daily minimum wet and dirty diapers
- You see blood in the baby's stool
- Your baby's stool is still brown/green after day 5
- Your baby's stool is white – this could indicate a problem with your baby's liver or gallbladder
- Baby is projectile vomiting – this could indicate a problem with your baby's stomach

- You see white spots in baby's mouth or on the tongue – this could indicate thrush, a fungal infection
- You find your baby is uncomfortable when lying flat and is arching his/her back – this could indicate problems with acid reflux

Sleeping

Twinkle twinkle little star, how I wonder what you are...

In this chapter we are going to talk about sleep. We are going to discuss normal sleep habits, evening sleep, how to get your baby to sleep, safe sleep, co-sleeping, and sleep schedules.

Normal Sleep Habits

Childbirth is a difficult and long process, not just for you, but also for baby! It really tires them out. **For the first 24 hours, the baby will mostly sleep and wake only for feedings.** Then, expect your **newborn to sleep about 16-18 hours a day.** Why does a newborn sleep so much? Brain development and neural connections are made during sleep. A newborn baby is exposed to so much environmental stimuli that it needs to sleep to register all that information in their brain. Also, during sleep, hormones are released, including the growth hormone, so that the baby can grow. Your baby will grow at a very fast rate, so, it needs lots of rest and energy to grow. When do you expect your baby to wake up? Expect a newborn to wake up every 2-3 hours. Newborns have small stomachs. I am talking about the size of a cherry. You will feed your baby, but it has such a small stomach that it empties fast, and baby is hungry again. Also, breastmilk is quickly digested, so baby will feel hungry again in 2-3 hours. As babies get older, their stomachs get bigger and they can hold more milk. The total hours of sleep in 24 hours is about 16 hours and frequency of waking is every 2-3 hours. What about awake time? When the baby wakes from a nap, the routine usually goes like this: offer a feeding, change the diaper, playtime and snuggle time, offer a feeding, change the diaper, then sleep time. This routine may last 30 minutes to 1 hour. This is how long the newborn can stay awake until it becomes sleepy again. Do not think that you can keep a newborn awake for a longer period and that the baby then will sleep longer on the next nap. This is counterproductive because **if the baby does not get its nap at the regular interval, they will be overtired and even harder to put to sleep**. As your baby gets older, he/she will be able to stay awake for longer. **Babies usually start to sleep for longer stretches of 5-6 hours once they become two months old**.

Evening Sleep Time

The newborn period is a time where your own sleep will be broken, and my rule is to try to **get at least one three hour or more stretch of sleep in a 24-hour period**. I want to give you some advice about evening sleep (or bedtime) that I found helped me with my children. **When babies are born, they do not have a day-night awareness**. You can help your baby develop their day-night cycle. The key is to make sure that **during the evening you keep stimulation low**. When the baby wakes in the night, the first thing you should do is offer a feeding. You may find that after a feeding, it may be diaper change time. This is because the **gastrointestinal tract becomes activated on feeding and will stimulate the baby to have a bowel movement**. If you are changing the baby's diaper in the evening, try not to put on the bedroom light. Use a nightlight to keep the room dark. You can also use a light that runs on batteries and goes on if you press the top part of it. I had one and my husband and I actually called it the "diaper light". It allowed us to change the baby's diaper without stimulating them with a bright light. I purchased a **wipe warmer** to help with nighttime diaper changes. You plug it into an electrical outlet and place the wipes in the container and it warms the wipes! I started using this because I found that when I wiped my baby's bum with a cold wipe, she woke up! Then, it would take double or triple the time to put her back to sleep. Also, if you are undressing the baby then try to cover the exposed parts with a blanket, again to make sure the baby doesn't get too cold and wake up.

Another thing I avoided at nighttime was too much auditory stimulation. I tried not to talk to the baby during these night wakings. If the baby was crying intolerably then yes of course, start to say something to soothe them but keep your volume low.

One last thing I will mention here is that you will hear stories where mothers say, "my newborn would sleep through the night!", "she didn't wake up for 8 hours straight". I will tell you that a baby needs to feed. If your newborn has gone more than 3 hours without feeding, then wake the baby up and feed them. The baby needs the calories from the milk to supply the brain with the energy for development. Sometimes, newborns become jaundiced when they don't drink enough milk in the early days so its important to make sure they are feeding every 2-3 hours. To help you keep track in the beginning, you can note the time when the baby started the feeding and then count 2-3 hours after that.

How to Get Your Baby to Sleep

Why does every book or article out there talk about "putting your baby to sleep" or "getting your baby to sleep"? Well, the reason is that babies need help falling asleep. Some babies, you will hear, go to sleep on their own. This is quite possible. Once you see that the baby is drowsy, you can try to lay them in their crib and they may doze off on their own. I applaud your baby if they can do this. They have good control of their sleep. However, most babies are not able to do this and require some help to fall asleep. When you were pregnant, the baby could fall asleep easily. It had a warm room (your uterus filled with warm amniotic fluid), darkness, muffled sounds of shushing and your heartbeat, tightness/compression feeling (due to small space), and it was rocked when you were walking.

First, make sure your baby is fed and diaper is changed. Your little one will not go to sleep easily if they are hungry or have a wet or soiled diaper. Once those are complete, then consider swaddling your newborn. Swaddling is a way to tighten a blanket on a baby so that they feel tight and secure. It replicates what they felt in the womb. There are swaddling blankets that you can use and there are ready swaddle products where you place the baby in and Velcro is used to tighten the blanket around the baby. Some babies will not like to be swaddled. Make sure you swaddle with the arms out.

All the following will help your baby fall asleep: rocking them gently in your arms, singing to them, keeping them close to your body, some may fall asleep while feeding, laying with them until they get into a deeper sleep, rocking them in a rocking chair, singing to them, putting on a musical lullaby, doing a "shushing" sound or use a sleep machine and the list goes on. You have to do what feels right to you to get your baby to sleep. It is such a satisfying feeling once your baby falls asleep. Your rocking or singing worked and now your little one is sound asleep! You can place them into their bassinet or crib once they have fallen asleep. If the baby is in a deep sleep, when you move them, they should not wake up. Some babies take longer to get into a deep sleep (20-30 minutes) and these are the babies where as soon as you put them down, they wake up. It means they were not in a deep state of sleep yet and felt that they have left your arms. If your baby wakes when you try to put them down, then try to get them back to sleep. Remember, they need the sleep to grow! Again, you will hear about the extremes – "my baby goes to sleep on their own, I just put them in the crib and leave the room" and "I had to rock my baby for the entire two hours so that they could stay asleep". Every baby is different, and you will have to adjust to their sleep habits. Most newborns can stay awake 1 hour or maximum 2 hours and then will need a nap.

How to Settle an Overtired Baby

If your baby has gone past naptime or evening bedtime, then it will be harder to put your baby to sleep. Let's say you have done everything mentioned above to try to get the baby to sleep and the baby is still crying. The baby will cry because of frustration. The baby wants to sleep but can't fall asleep. My advice at this point is to be persistent in whichever method you use to put your baby to sleep. The baby will cry but keep on doing your rocking, singing or the technique you use. I promise you, your little one will fall asleep! I remember trying to put my overtired baby to sleep and it was so difficult! Just be persistent in your sleeping method and soon your baby will be fast asleep.

Safe Sleep

This is the most important section in this chapter. Safe Sleep! You should follow safe sleep instructions in order to help prevent SIDS – Sudden Infant Death Syndrome. This sounds scary so let me explain it to you and give you the information so that you can do everything to prevent it. SIDS happens in infants less than one-year-old. **To help reduce the risk of SIDS you should not smoke during or after pregnancy**.

Do not let anyone else smoke in the home or around your baby. Smoke contains chemicals, including carcinogens that are cancer causing chemicals, that can leech into clothing and skin. If your partner or you smoke, make sure you change clothing or wipe down your skin before holding the baby. If you or your partner smoke then please consider speaking to your doctors about ways to quit smoking.

Let's go through what consists of a safe sleeping environment. **Put the baby on their back to sleep, no pillows, no blankets, no hats, no bumpers, no stuffed animals, room temperature between 20 to 22 degrees Celsius (68 – 71.6 degrees Fahrenheit), do not overdress the baby, have the baby in their crib in your bedroom at least for the first six months (co-rooming), and use a pacifier.** Using a pacifier decreases the risk of SIDS. **Do not let your newborn sleep in the car seat.** In the car seat the baby's neck is flexed where it can limit their breathing. If your baby falls asleep in the car seat, remove as soon as possible and put them on their back in the crib. Always put the baby on their back to sleep. Placing them on their stomach could limit their ability to breathe. You do not want anything in the crib that could possibly cover the baby's face and prevent them from breathing. Swaddle blankets with Velcro or with zippers are great products because the baby cannot kick it off themselves. You want the room to be cool and not too warm. Never overdress a baby. The general rule is **the baby needs one more layer than you.** A short sleeve onesie underneath their pyjamas is good enough. **Do not put a hat on the baby** when it is sleeping. Babies release heat from their head so a hat can keep that extra heat in their body. **Breastfeeding has been associated with less risk of SIDS**. There is lots of controversy about whether you should let a newborn use a pacifier because it may cause nipple confusion and then the baby will not take the breast. I have found that there is low risk of nipple confusion and the pacifier helps to soothe the baby. **My advice is to use a pacifier to help soothe the baby**. Also, you want good air flow and new air full of oxygen in your living space – so air out your living space once a day. Open the windows and let that stale air out to help decrease risk of SIDS.

It is not safe to co-sleep (baby to be in your bed) because of risk of suffocation to the baby. You or your partner may roll on the baby or your bedding or pillows may not let your baby get enough air and good oxygen flow. Co-rooming is much safer than co-sleeping. Having the baby's crib in the same room as mom has many benefits including decreasing risk of SIDS, helps with bonding, and easier nighttime feedings. You can put the crib right up against your side of the bed. Newborn babies love being close to mom. They love being able to smell mom (so no perfumes or deodorants!). They love feeling mom breathe on them. You will find your baby will be more content when they are close to you. They need to know that their mother – the one that brought them into this world – is there for them during their new journey into this life.

Newborns may have some irregular breathing patterns as they learn how to use their lungs in their new world. They may take a deep breath at times, sigh, or take a fast breath. What you can do is monitor your baby if he/she begins to breathe differently – watch for continued abnormal breathing patterns, lethargy, blue lips/face or hands/feet and if any of these happen then seek medical attention immediately.

If you have a premature baby (born before 37 weeks) and are worried about their breathing at nighttime, there are oxygen saturation monitors that you can purchase. These are placed on the baby's foot and can alert you if their oxygen is low or their heart rate goes too high or low. Premature babies are at higher risk of SIDS and may have irregular breathing due to prematurity.

Safe Sleep Tips

- **Keep room temperature 20 - 22 degrees Celsius** (68 – 71.6 degrees Fahrenheit)

- No blankets/bumpers/pillows/toys in the crib
- No hats
- No smoking around the baby and in the home
- Do not overdress the baby
- Use a pacifier
- Keep the baby's bed in your room for the first 6 months
- Use a sleeper as a blanket
- Always put the baby on its back to sleep
- Do not let the baby sleep in car seat for an extended time

Sleep Schedules

I put this section into this chapter as a sarcasm of sorts. You will read books where they talk about putting your baby onto a schedule. Let me tell you now, you cannot put your baby onto a schedule! It is a baby and it is unpredictable! Again, do what feels right for you and your baby. The baby is smart and will give you signals when it is hungry or sleepy. The first six weeks are a hectic time and the newborn cannot be on a sleep schedule. After your little one turns two months old, his/her sleep pattern will become more predictable and you both will be getting more sleep.

Changing, Bathing, & Skin

Changing Diapers

Let's talk diapers! Essentially, you should get excited when you see a dirty diaper because it means your baby is getting enough to drink and their gastrointestinal tract is working well! I recommend, especially for new mothers, to track how many wet and dirty diapers your newborn baby has. Ok, so let's take it from the top. Your baby has been in the womb for nine months floating in amniotic fluid. It doesn't know how it feels to be "wet". When your newborn has a wet diaper or dirty diaper, then their skin in the area will start to feel cold. You will find the baby more uncomfortable and it may start to cry because it doesn't like that cold feeling. Some parents may have purchased a change table. This is alright to use as long as you secure the baby on the table with the safety belt. Change tables are convenient because you can store all the materials you need on it. If you do not have a change table, then you could purchase a changing pad and use this on a hard surface, such as the top of your bed or even the floor. A changing pad is a water-resistant pad. Always have this open and ready.

You have placed the baby on the pad, now what's next? I recommend having all the materials on the go and ready. I will tell you why. Once you open that baby's diaper, things have to move fast because they could easily urinate some more or poop some more and you need to be ready! After having my baby, at the beginning of each day I would make my bed and get the "changing area" ready, which included having the change pad, diapers, and diaper cream ready. The wipes were ready in the wipe warmer. So, again, you have the baby on the changing pad. Now, open the diaper cream container and open the clean diaper and get it ready for use. Get the wipes ready. Open the dirty diaper and grab your baby's feet in your left hand (if you are right handed). If you don't grab your baby's feet, then most likely the feet will end up in the poop! Bring your baby's feet upwards towards their head so you can expose their bottom. Use those wipes to clean the baby's bottom. Your other option, of course, is to wash their bottom with mild soap and warm water and dry with a towel. Sometimes, I would wipe the baby's bottom and still wash it with soap and water to make sure it was clean. Baby wipes on a newborn's skin can sometimes cause a red rash on their bottom. I recommend rinsing the wipes with water before use. I recommend purchasing unscented wipes.

Now, the baby's bottom is clean and the important step here is to get that clean diaper right under their bum quickly. If you don't, you may easily be left with a mess to clean up. They may urinate or have another bowel movement before you put the clean diaper on them! This has happened to me on more than one occasion, so I am teaching you now to beware and get that clean diaper on fast!

I always get this question from parents: how much diaper cream do I put on? My response is: make sure you cover all the areas where urine might touch their skin and put a medium thickness layer. This is one of the main ways you will prevent diaper rash. The other way is by changing their diaper frequently. If you leave a wet diaper for a long time on a baby, then the baby will experience skin breakdown in the area due to high moisture on the skin. High moisture can allow bacteria and/or fungus to grow. The maximum amount of time a baby can stay with a wet diaper depends on the brand of diaper used. Higher quality diapers have super-absorbent materials that will keep the baby dry for longer. If your baby has had a bowel movement, it is recommended to change it immediately.

Which diaper cream to use is also a common question. Diaper cream contains zinc oxide which is a very good skin barrier cream. Zinc oxide is the substance that mountain climbers and skiers put on the tips of their noses so that they don't get sunburn. You can use it on your skin too at the beach to prevent sunburn. The average zinc oxide content in diaper creams is 10%. Different products may have a higher content, and these would work even better to prevent diaper rash. Petroleum ointment (Vaseline) is also a very good barrier cream that can be applied to the baby's bottom.

Make sure you have all the materials ready before opening that dirty diaper – your changing pad, clean diaper opened and ready, diaper rash cream opened, and wipes. Remember to always wash your hands after changing a baby's diaper. **New mothers are prone to hand dermatitis because of frequent handwashing**. Make sure you moisturize frequently with a non-perfumed moisturizer. Another thing I will mention is that you should have a small bottle filled with laundry detergent on the ready. If your baby has a bowel movement or urinates on bedding or clothing, it is best to **clean the stain right away with warm water and laundry detergent**. Baby's stools can stain clothing and bedding permanently if not cleaned immediately.

Just a reminder here about night wakings and diaper changes – don't stimulate the baby too much as to wake them – do not speak to them (only softly if you must), no bright lights (use the "diaper light") and use warm wipes on their bottoms.

Diaper rash is a red rash on your baby's bottom. Again, it can be prevented by applying a good amount of diaper cream on the baby's bottom and by performing frequent diaper changes. Sometimes the rash will become bright red and may get worse as time goes on. If this is the case, then you may require a prescription cream to help get rid of the rash. Take your baby to the doctor for examination of the rash.

When you change your baby's diaper you will have a good visualization of the genitalia. In males, you will see the scrotal sac, but it may not have a definite outline of the testicles. The doctor will have to examine to make sure both testicles are in the scrotum. In females, you may notice the vulva, the skin outside of the vaginal opening to be swollen. This is a normal response to the mother's hormones. This swelling will decrease in 1-2 weeks. Some female babies will have some clear or yellow vaginal discharge in the first few days. You can wipe gently on the vulva and spread the vulva gently to wipe the area. Make sure you wipe off any stool that may get into the vulva area. The vaginal discharge will go away on its own. It also is a response from the mother's hormones. A newborn baby girl may also have a small amount of vaginal bleeding around day 2-10 of life. This is technically their "first period". It is a vaginal bleed due to a mother's hormones and is normal. If you have any concerns about your baby's genitalia, make sure you ask your doctor.

Changing a baby's diaper is a perfect opportunity to get in some tummy time. Tummy time is where you place your baby on its belly and give him/her an opportunity to lift his/her head off the floor. You should do this 2-3 times a day for at least 2-3 minutes at a time. Some babies will begin to cry, so stop the session and try again later. Tummy time will help your baby's neck muscles and shoulders become stronger. It contributes to their motor development. Don't forget to get in that tummy time!

Bathing & Skin

When your tiny bundle of joy is born, it is born with a white layer over its skin called vernix. This layer has two functions. One is to keep the baby warm during the time after birth and second, it acts to provide another barrier for the skin. This helps keep the skin moisturized and protect it from infection. After your baby is born, the hospital nurses usually give the baby a bath. In the hospitals, you will observe that the nurse will likely use a bath support in the tub and/or use towels/sponges to wash the baby. I highly recommend purchasing a bath support. Caution! Newborn babies are slippery when wet! Once you go home with baby, you are going to have to give your baby a bath. If you have a baby boy and he was circumcised, then do not give him a bath until day five after the circumcision. You can give your baby boy a sponge bath.

Different books say different things in terms of frequency of baths. Giving your baby a bath every other day is ok. Use your judgement – so if your baby has vomited/spit-up that day or had a large bowel movement, or it has been a summer day and the baby has been sweating – then feel free to wash more often.

Let's go through the steps to bathe your baby. Firstly, have all your materials ready. This includes: bath tub and bath support, baby towel, baby shampoo/body wash, rinse cup/jug, bath thermometer, and the changing pad ready with a new set of clothes and diaper ready. Make sure the water is the right temperature by using bath thermometer. If you do not have one, place your elbow in the water and the water should be warm, not hot. Normal bath temperature is around 37 degrees Celsius (98.6 Fahrenheit). Fill the tub about 1-2 inches with water and fill your rinse cup/jug. If you have a bath support, then place the baby on the support. Will your baby like the water? Some babies love the water and just sit back, relax, and enjoy their bath. Most babies will not like the feeling and will cry. Try to sing to your baby or talk them through what is going on, so they know you are there. If you do not have a bath support, then it can get tricky. If you have someone who can help you with bath time, then you can hold your baby with both hands and the other person can bathe the baby. If you don't have any help to bathe the baby and you do not have a bath support, then the easiest way is to take your non-dominant hand and let your baby's head rest on your forearm/wrist and you grab its shoulder with your thumb and fingers. The baby's bum can rest on the tub and you can use your dominant hand to bathe the baby. You can do the same hold when you need to clean the baby's back.

How do you bathe the baby? You can use towels, sponges, or none of these. You do not have to use a large amount of the shampoo or baby wash. Dispense only a small coin sized amount into the palm of your hand. I want to share a trick I have learned with my children. I did use bath supports and when I would place the baby on the bath support, they always cried. I think it was because they felt cold. I would have small towels ready in the water and once the baby was on the bath support, I would open the towel and put it on their body. This kept the baby warm and baby would stop crying! Your baby is in the tub, you have the shampoo in the palm of your hand, but where do you start? It doesn't matter but **make sure you clean between the baby's folds**. Your baby's folds can hold moisture and can develop a rash like a diaper rash. Common folds are the neck and thighs. You can spread the folds during the day to let them air dry. You can wipe gently with a towel that is wet with warm water and mild soap. Make sure you dry the area well! Another trick that I used to do with my babies is put diaper cream in the folds! If you see a red rash in the folds, take your baby to the doctor for assessment. There have been cases where a serious skin infection can develop in the folds or in the diaper area. Monitor the skin in-between your baby's folds.

You can lather the baby's hair with shampoo also but if there are pieces of hard substances on the top of the baby's head, do not try to clean it off – this is **cradle cap**. This will come off the baby's head on its own. It may take up to one year until its fully removed. It does not harm the baby and is present because of overactive sweat glands. Other skin issues you may notice when giving your baby a bath is in the belly button area. Once the umbilical cord is cut there will be a stump remaining that will eventually fall off, but this may take up to three weeks. You can wash the stump gently but do not pull on the stump. That may cause pain for the baby. You should be concerned if there is yellow or green discharge coming from the umbilical stump, a foul odour, or redness around the area. Make sure you show this to the doctor.

Two other things I will mention here are skin mottling and acrocyanosis. Skin mottling is when you will notice string-like red marks on your baby's skin. You will notice it when the baby is cold – this is normal! This is just the change in blood flow when your baby's skin is exposed to cold temperature. Acrocyanosis is when a newborn's hands and feet look blue. This can be scary for new parents, but it is normal, and the blue colour will fade within the first 1-2 weeks of birth.

A colour that is concerning on the baby's skin is yellow. This could indicate jaundice. If the baby's skin is yellow or carrot coloured, or the whites of the eyes have turned yellow – this is jaundice. Jaundice occurs when there is too much bilirubin in the baby's blood. Some babies get jaundice at day 2 or 3 of life and most of the time it is not harmful. Your doctor may repeat your baby's blood test to check the bilirubin level. If the level is too high, then your baby may need phototherapy. Phototherapy is where the baby goes under special lights that help the baby's body get rid of the extra bilirubin.

The best way you can help your baby get rid of extra bilirubin is to feed your baby often. Some babies that are jaundiced will require formula supplementation. This way your baby can urinate the extra bilirubin. Just a quick review. Jaundice can be caused by the baby being born too early, infection, bruising from birth, and not feeding well. Two main types of jaundice include physiological (common one, improves on its own with feeding of the baby) and pathological (high bilirubin levels). In Ontario, Canada, it is standard that every baby gets their bilirubin checked before leaving the hospital. This blood test is usually done at 24 hours of life.

Let's get back to the steps for bathing your baby. You have cleaned all the baby folds, gently cleaned the umbilical stump, and now you are ready to rinse the baby. Use the rinse cup/jug and pour the water gently over the baby. Make sure to not pour the water so that a large volume will run on the baby's face. The baby will not react well if water is poured on its face and it is dangerous because the baby may get water into its mouth and not swallow it in time. Please be careful when rinsing your baby. Now, use the baby towel to wrap the baby and bath time is done! Good job! The baby is going to feel cold when you start to dry them, so they will start to cry. Have your pacifier ready to help soothe the baby. Pat the baby dry and make sure you dry all the folds of the baby. Make sure you pat dry the baby's neck and yes, they might start to cry when you try to move their head back to get to that neck!

Once the baby is dry the next question is, do I apply baby moisturizer? I will tell you that in the first six weeks the baby's skin is very sensitive to any lotions. If you do want to apply lotion, make sure you use hypoallergenic and/or unscented moisturizer. It is not necessary to moisturize after a bath. Where it may be necessary is if your baby has eczema. Eczema is very dry skin that comes in patches and may cause itchiness for the baby. Eczema can run in families. If you notice these dry skin patches, then feel free to moisturize the baby after bath time. Petroleum ointment, aka Vaseline, is a very good moisturizer and I highly recommend it. I always recommend petroleum ointment to all my patients who have eczema or suffer from dry skin. Sometimes this is all you need to heal the skin and give it an extra layer of protection.

If you do decide to moisturize the baby's skin after a bath, then I recommend you have some fun with your baby. Put on a nice tune and give your baby a relaxing massage. Babies can get tense too, especially because they are trying to learn how to live in this new world. When dressing the baby, remember he/she needs one more extra layer that adults. Usually, bedtime is easier and runs more smoothly as a bath can tire the baby, make them more relaxed, and get them into sleep mode. Baby bath shampoos/wash with lavender can help soothe them into a good night's sleep.

If you decide to circumcise your baby boy, then please read this section. After the circumcision there are some things you can do to help the penis heal. After the circumcision, a small dressing is placed over the penis so that it does not directly touch the diaper. When you change the diaper, gently remove the small dressing and gently pour clean water over the penis to help clean it. Pat the area dry very gently. Next, take a small piece of gauze and place a small amount of petroleum ointment on it and place it loosely around the penis. The petroleum ointment will make sure the dressing does not stick to the penis. After the first 24 hours you can stop placing a dressing on the area but continue to place petroleum ointment on the diaper area where the penis will come in contact with the diaper. Continue to do this until the penis has healed in 4-5 days. Do not give your baby a bath until the penis is healed. Make sure you see your doctor if you notice any abnormal discharge, redness, fever, swelling in the area. Also, if your baby boy has trouble passing urine or has decreased wet diapers then see a doctor immediately. A small amount of bleeding is normal right after circumcision but if it continues call your doctor immediately. Lastly, a yellowish, sticky hard substance may appear on head of penis on day 2-3 after circumcision, this is normal and do not attempt to remove. It will fall off on its own.

Changing a baby's diaper, giving your baby a bath, and taking care of all baby's skin needs will get easier with time. I hope this chapter has given you the tips needed for successful diaper changes and baths.

When to Seek Medical Attention…

- Red rash on buttocks and diaper cream is not resolving the rash
- Red rash in the baby's folds
- Concerns regarding baby's genitalia
- Dry skin patches on baby's skin
- Discharge, foul odour, redness from the umbilical stump
- In baby boys that are circumcised – any discharge, fever, foul odour, redness at the penis, not having enough wet diapers or having a decrease in urine output

- Baby's skin is yellow, or carrot coloured, or the whites of the eyes have turned yellow – this is jaundice.

Crying

Hush little baby don't you cry…

Welcome to the Crying Chapter! This is the thing I find new parents are most worried about: crying. I always see new parents bringing their babies to me with concerns of *"Why is my baby crying?"*, *"Why won't my baby stop crying?"*, and *"What can I do to get my baby to stop crying?"*. I want to prepare you in full, so you know what to do if your baby is crying. Let's jump into it…

Why Does My Baby Cry?

I want you to put yourself into your baby's shoes. You have been living for nine months in a home that is warm, dark, and soft. You can hear a shushing sound (mother's blood flow) and your mother's heartbeat sound and both are soothing. You can hear and smell your mother – the person who is keeping you safe in your home. You are easily put to sleep because it is warm, dark, tight, and your mother's walking is rocking you to sleep. Your food comes directly to you, so you do not need to work for your food. Your urine is mixed with the amniotic fluid, so you don't feel it wet on your body. There is no stranger who is holding you, only your mother keeping you safe. There are no loud noises or bright lights… it sounds like something every adult wants to do on their vacation!

When you go into labour, this is where your baby's life starts to change, or should I say get harder. As your uterus begins to contract, the baby is feeling those contractions. Labour and delivery are exhausting not only to you but also to the baby. Once the baby comes into this world, its life totally changes. He/she needs to adjust to its new environment – loud noises, bright lights, variations in temperature, wet feeling on its buttock, and mother is not skin-to-skin 24 hours a day. The baby also needs to work now to eat. Again, feeding is a process that is new to the baby and it does take energy to feed. Sucking uses lots of muscles and can be tiring to the baby. Having a bowel movement is something new to the baby also. When the baby is in the uterus the gastrointestinal tract is on temporary hold. The first bowel movements for the baby may give the baby abdominal cramping and this new feeling is scary to the baby. All these things give the baby a reason to cry! Another thing crying is used for is **communication**. It is your baby's *only* method of communication to you. Crying is normal and is part of your baby's growth and development. It is a good sign that your baby cries when it needs something or dislikes something. Another **good sign is that your baby's cry is a strong and loud cry**. If your baby is crying and you think it is a soft, whimpering cry or a shrieking cry, then this is concerning and make sure you see a doctor.

Baby's crying will follow a developmental pattern. This is called the "crying curve". The amount of crying seems to increase at 2-3 weeks, **peaks at 6-8 weeks**, and then gradually declines. This is the pattern for the first three months of the baby's life. All babies cry. Even crying for several hours of a day is normal. It is the baby's way of telling you that it needs something. Your crying baby may be hungry (most common cause), tired, overstimulated, needs a diaper change, bored, needs to feel close to mommy, in pain, or the baby may be sick. A baby can be in pain if they need to burp, need to pass gas, or need to have a bowel movement. The baby can be in pain from something more medically serious too, however, this would cause inconsolable crying for hours.

Colic is a term used to describe a baby that cries several hours a day and is difficult to soothe. It is found now that this **intense crying, colic, is a normal variation**. The important thing to do when you think your baby has colic is to take them to their doctor for a check-up. Babies can cry intensely if they are in pain or have an infection. If you have a thermometer, you can check their temperature. A fever is a temperature over 38 degrees Celsius (over 100.4 Fahrenheit). If your newborn has a fever, you must take them to the doctor for an examination. Sometimes, an infection early in life can be serious because your baby has not had any vaccinations and its immune system is brand new. We will talk more about this in the *When to Seek Medical Attention* Chapter. The most common reason your baby will cry is because he/she is hungry. If the baby is still crying after you feed him/her, then follow the step-by-step checklist below.

Crying Step-by-Step Checklist

- Is the baby hungry? Put the baby on the breast or offer formula and burp the baby
- Does the baby have a wet or soiled diaper? Change the diaper
- Is the baby sleepy or overtired? Put the baby to sleep
- Does the baby have a fever? Check the baby's temperature. If the baby has a fever seek medical attention immediately

- At this point, if you answer "No" to all the above, then you should try to comfort the baby by cuddling, hugging, rocking, skin-to-skin contact, offer a pacifier, reduce noise and bright lights, swaddle the baby, give the baby a bath – If these things don't work then seek medical attention

How to Calm Your Baby

In this section, we will go through different things that you can try to help calm your crying baby. First, try to meet your baby's needs. Check if your baby is hungry by offering a feeding. Check if the baby needs a diaper change. Be aware of when the baby woke from his/her nap. The baby may be tired or overtired and now its naptime. If the baby is overtired and crying, whatever technique/soothing method you use, continue it until your baby is asleep. You can review sleep and overtiredness in the *Sleeping* chapter. Offering a pacifier can help soothe the baby. Check if your baby needs burping. If you think your baby has gas you can move his/her legs in a bicycle motion to help move that gastrointestinal tract to help pass the gas. Check your baby's temperature to make sure they do not have a fever. Different movements can help to calm your crying baby, these include gently rocking your baby, walking with your baby, taking your baby on a stroller ride or car ride, or placing them in a baby swing. Try to imitate the rocking motion that the baby felt when he/she was in the womb. Sitting in a rocking chair with the baby also can help calm them. Swaddling is another thing you can do. Swaddling mimics the tight feeling of the uterus that the baby is used to. Soothing noises such as making a shushing sound, singing, playing soft music, vacuum or fan sounds, and static noise. You can reduce noise and darken the room also to imitate the womb. Skin-to-skin contact with your baby also imitates the closeness the baby felt with you in the womb. Bathing the baby can help calm the baby because of the warm water feeling on its skin. Stroking or gently massaging your baby can help also. All of these are suggestions to help calm your crying baby. Remember, sometimes these techniques may work some of the time, but they will not work all the time.

If you do not respond to a baby's cry, it will feel neglected. **Continued neglect can have a serious impact on your child's mental health. You cannot spoil your baby by responding to its cries.** The baby needs you to respond to its cries so that it can form normal emotional relationships with you and with others in the future.

Feeling Frustrated

Feeling frustrated? As a new mother you are supposed to be elated with joy, right? Well, yes, until crying gets in the way. **Long periods of crying can be *very stressful* to a parent.** You will feel frustrated, helpless, and angry. You may feel like you are a bad mother because you cannot get your baby to stop crying. Remember that your baby is trying to adjust to its new life. Most importantly, remember that crying is a part of your baby's normal development. A baby is going to cry. It is not your fault! In the sections above, we went through reasons that your baby may be crying, and we went through ways to soothe your baby. If you have checked all the reasons and tried all the ways… and your baby is still crying, this can be frustrating. The baby will be ok. What should you do? You should put the baby in the crib, walk away, and **take a 5-10 minute break**. This is perfectly fine to do. Then you will feel a bit refreshed and will be ready to take care of the baby again. Every baby has a different temperament, and this will determine its crying personality. In my experience, when I had my children, there was a maximum time of crying tolerability and this was two hours. After two hours, *you must take a break*. Either do what I mentioned above by leaving the baby in the crib and taking a 10-minute break or let your partner or a family member hold the baby so that you can take a break. The most important thing is for you to *Take a Break*! "But Dr. Doko", you say, "I am the mother of this baby and I should be able to tolerate the crying". I am telling you, **it is normal to feel frustrated with your baby when it is crying**! Take a break! If the baby is crying and you are getting frustrated, the baby senses this. In turn, it will become even harder to soothe. Taking a break is beneficial to you and the baby.

Shaken Baby Syndrome

I am urging you to take a break when taking care of a crying baby because if you don't, there can be dreadful consequences. Parents that do not take a break may have the urge to shake their baby. They shake their baby because they are frustrated and angry and just want the baby to stop crying. NEVER SHAKE YOUR BABY! NEVER SHAKE YOUR BABY! NEVER SHAKE YOUR BABY! I cannot stress this enough. If you shake your baby, you will cause something called Shaken Baby Syndrome. **Shaking a baby causes disturbance in the tissues of the brain**. This can lead to **permanent brain damage** that can cause blindness, learning disabilities, seizures, strokes, and physical disabilities. Shaking a baby can also be fatal. There have been national campaigns educating the public about Shaken Baby Syndrome. Due to this, the incidence of it has gone down. If you get to the point where you feel like you want to shake your baby – it is time for a break! Put the baby in the crib or give the baby to your partner or family member and take minimum 5-10-minute break so that you can feel rested and take care of your precious baby again.

When to Seek Medical Attention...

- If your baby has a soft, whimpering cry or a loud, shrieking cry
- If your baby is snoring
- Inconsolable crying that has been going on nonstop for over 3 hours – take your child to the doctor – they may have an infection or be in pain

When to Seek Medical Attention

As a family physician, I take care of patients of all ages. It is a privilege to be able to take care of my youngest patients, the newborns. After taking care of my patient during her pregnancy, it is a delight to see them come in with the new addition to their family! That first visit with the newborn is one of many during our patient-doctor relationship.

This chapter is dedicated to teaching you when to seek medical attention. In the Chapter titled "Caring for Yourself", I did make notes throughout the chapter of instances where you should seek medical attention. I will do the same thing in this chapter and will divide it by topics. When I say, "seek medical attention", I mean make sure you see a doctor. If your family doctor's office is not open, you need to make sure you can see a doctor, and this may mean going to a walk-in clinic or the emergency room. If you ever have any concern, whether it is for yourself or your baby, make sure you tell your doctor.

When to Seek Medical Attention... The Mother

Pregnancy

- 5-1-1 Rule: If you are having contractions that are 5 minutes apart, lasting 1 minute, and this has been going on for over 1 hour then you are in labour!

- If you have <u>any</u> vaginal bleeding * if you have profuse vaginal bleeding, then you need to call the ambulance

- If your water breaks

- If you have not felt the baby move for over 2 hours

- If you experience any of the following: chest pain, shortness of breath, calf pain, headache, abdominal pain, fever, rash on skin, dizziness, numbness or tingling in your body, blurry vision, extreme itchiness, bleeding after intercourse

Giving Birth… Perineum & General Health

- If you are experiencing severe pain in perineum that is not relieved by your pain medications
- If you are experiencing severe abdominal pain
- If you are experiencing foul smelling vaginal discharge
- If you are experiencing burning on urination, increased frequency of urination, blood in the urine, pain on the sides of your back
- If you experience a fever (temperature $\geq$ 38°C)
- If you experience a fever (temperature $\geq$ 38°C) especially with any of the following: perineum pain, foul vaginal discharge, severe

abdominal pain, pain on urination, leg pain, headache

- If you are soaking one or more pad per hour, passing clots, and/or passing bright red blood
- If you are having redness, swelling, tenderness, or pain in your legs
- If you are experiencing chest pain, shortness of breath, dizziness, blurry vision, headache, nausea, vomiting, rash

C-Section

- If you have any of the following at your C-section incision site: redness, swelling, drainage, foul odour, opening of the wound, or increasing pain, with or without fever

Gastrointestinal Health

- You have gone 5 days without a bowel movement

- You have hemorrhoids that do not improve with the creams applied
- You have hemorrhoids that are causing severe pain
- You are having bright red blood from the rectum

Breast Health

- If your breasts are very painful, red, and you have a fever, this may mean you have an infection
- If you are having nipple pain – this may indicate nipple infection
- If you are having trouble breastfeeding – as this may give you breast pain and may affect the amount of milk your baby is receiving
- If you have pain on breastfeeding – as this could be a sign of infection or trouble with feeding technique

Deep Venous Thrombosis

- You have pain, redness, fever, and/or swelling in your calf
- If you experience shortness of breath and/or chest pain, cough, coughing up blood - this may indicate a pulmonary embolism

Headache

- Headache that does not get better with acetaminophen and/or ibuprofen
- Headache that increases in severity or limits your function
- Headache associated with one or more of the following: fever, dizziness, changes in vision, numbness and/or tingling in the body, changes in speech, vomiting, nausea, weakness in the extremities

Mood

- If you experience any combination of the following, especially for more than two weeks: sad mood, decreased energy, decreased concentration, insomnia or hypersomnolence, loss in interest in usual activities/hobbies, feelings of guilt, decreased appetite, general overall feeling of being "slowed down", suicidal or homicidal thoughts, high anxiety

- Seek immediate attention if you have thoughts of harming yourself or baby or are having paranoia or hallucinations

When to Seek Medical Attention... The Baby

Dear mother, you will know if there is something wrong with your baby. It is the mother's instinct. If you have any worry, make sure you see the doctor.

If your newborn ever has a fever equal to or over 38 degrees Celsius (100.4 Fahrenheit), they *must* be seen by a doctor. Remember, newborns have a new immune system and have difficulty fighting off infections.

Obtain <u>Immediate Emergency Help</u> If your Baby

- Has difficulty breathing
- Turns a blue colour
- Loses consciousness, is unable to be awakened, or is limp or very lethargic with weak cry/whimpering cry
- Has seizures or convulsions
- Has injuries – bleeding, burn, fall, poisoning

These are all serious concerns that require a doctor's examination immediately. Do not hesitate, just call the ambulance.

Feeding & Baby's Digestive System

- Baby is not latching properly
- Baby is not feeding the minimum feeds per day
- Baby is not having required wet diapers a day
- Baby is too drowsy/sleepy/limp and may not feed to meet the minimum feedings a day and/or have the daily minimum wet and dirty diapers
- You see blood in the baby's stool
- Your baby's stool is still brown/green after day 5
- Your baby's stool is white – this could indicate a problem with your baby's liver or gallbladder
- Baby is projectile vomiting – this could indicate a problem with your baby's stomach

- You see white spots in baby's mouth or on the tongue – this could indicate thrush, a fungal infection
- You find your baby is uncomfortable when lying flat and is arching his/her back – this could indicate problems with acid reflux

Baby Sleep

- If you have any questions about baby sleep – what is safe, how to get the baby to sleep, your doctor can help answer these questions

Changing Diapers & Skin

- Red rash on buttocks and diaper cream is not resolving the rash
- Red rash in the baby's folds
- Concerns regarding baby's genitalia
- Dry skin patches on baby's skin

- Discharge, foul odour, redness from the umbilical stump
- In baby boys that are circumcised – any discharge, fever, foul odour, redness at the penis, not having enough wet diapers or having a decrease in urine output
- Baby's skin is yellow, or carrot coloured, or the whites of the eyes have turned yellow – this is jaundice.

Crying

- If your baby has a soft, whimpering cry or a loud, shrieking cry
- If your baby is snoring
- Inconsolable crying that has been going on for over 3 hours – take your child to the doctor – they may have an infection or be in pain

Regular Doctor's Visits

Mother's Check-Ups

If everything is going well, as a new mother, you will need your postpartum check at the six-week mark. This can be done at your family doctor's office or your obstetrician.

The postpartum visit for the mother may review the following:

- Review the type of delivery
- Breastfeeding concerns
- Bowel and bladder function
- Perineal concerns
- Vaginal discharge concerns
- Whether you require a rubella vaccine booster or any other vaccines
- Whether you require a pap test

- Will check your blood pressure and heart rate

- May do a pelvic exam

- May perform a breast exam to check for any signs of infection

- Will ask about mood to screen for postpartum depression

- Will discuss continuing your prenatal vitamins during breastfeeding and preconceptual folate prior to next pregnancy (you should be taking minimum 1mg folic acid for at least 3 months before getting pregnant)

- Whether you require birth control and discuss options

- The doctor will ask you about your family and support network – being a new mother is hard and good support is essential

- The doctor will ask you about your relationship with your partner and screen you for relationship abuse – verbal, emotional, physical, and sexual

Baby's Check-Ups

You will be visiting the doctor with your newborn on multiple occasions for the well-baby care checks. They occur at the following ages: 1 week old, 2 weeks old, 1 month old, 2 months old, 4 months old, 6 months old, 9 months old, 12 months old, 15 months old, 18 months old, 2 years old and then yearly annual check-ups are recommended. This is the recommended visit schedule for Ontario, Canada. Now, these visits have multiple functions. They are a great way to check in with the mother to see how new motherhood is going. They are a way to make sure the baby is growing normally physically and developmentally. Additionally, the visits may coincide with times when immunizations are administered. Ask your doctor about any additional vaccines that your baby may qualify for.

Each doctor's visit for the baby will review…

- Baby's growth: length, weight, head circumference
- The parent's concerns about the baby
- Feeding method and amount of milk taken
- Vitamin D supplementation (required if breastfeeding and until the baby starts taking formula or cow's milk)
- Stool and urine pattern - # wet and dirty diapers
- Doctor will discuss injury prevention – for example car seat safety, carbon monoxide alarms, smoke alarms, bath temperature, safe sleep, smoking, sun exposure, locking up medicines & chemicals, no over the counter medicines for the baby unless discuss with doctor
- Baby's sleep patterns
- Bonding with the baby

- How is the mother coping with motherhood – screen for postpartum depression as the mother's emotional health affects the baby's emotional health
- Discuss baby development
- The doctor will examine the baby
- Doctor may administer immunizations if required

As we discussed above, if there are any instances where you need to seek medical attention for your baby – please call your doctor and do not hesitate to do so.

Don't Forget To…

I am writing this chapter to remind you that in this hectic time of having a new baby, there are some things you should not forget…

Savour Each Moment

Did I change the diaper? When was the last poopy diaper? More family are coming over! Did I put the clothes in the dryer? I have to soak the dirty onesie. More than a million things are going through your mind. I want to remind you to STOP, TAKE A DEEP, SLOW BREATH, and LOOK YOUR BABY IN THE EYES. Time will stop, and I want you to savour that moment. You will hear this phrase from so many other parents but first hear it from me – they grow up too fast! In the middle of your hectic day, don't forget to stop, breathe, and look your baby in the eyes. Savour it.

Remember it. Hold your baby close and feel the love between you and your baby. After doing this, you will feel refreshed and energized. Yes, there is always something to do, but you should savour the moments with your baby. Let time stop and just enjoy your baby!

Documenting & Saving Memories

Don't forget to document your memories with video recording and photographs. That baby is going to grow up so fast! Make sure you document that cute outfit, first smile, those tiny feet, and those chubby cheeks. Handprint and footprint kits are available also if you wanted to preserve your baby's prints. I will tell you that I have thousands of photographs of my children. I store them in an external digital hard drive and I print any photographs that have special meaning to me, just in case the digital file malfunctions. You should think about backing up your photograph and video files and printing some photographs. Memory books are also great ways to preserve memories. They are popular baby shower gifts, so you may not even need to buy one! You can always make one yourself too. In memory books, you can document notes about the pregnancy, delivery, and the baby's firsts. I even taped my daughter's hospital identification badge into her book. I taped the envelope from her first piece of mail (it was her birth certificate). I bought a pink box and made that her memory box. Inside I have placed her memory book, her going home outfit from the hospital, her dress from her first holiday party, and now things like her first drawings! Later, when your child grows up, the both of you could sit and browse the memory box together.

Bonding

When you are spending quality time with your baby – holding your baby, singing to it, rocking your baby, and more – you are bonding with your baby. Bonding is the long-term relationship built between parents and their baby. Bonding begins right after birth when the baby is placed on the mother's chest. Here are some tips on how to bond with your baby: singing, talking, holding them close to your body, taking care of your baby such as feeding, changing diapers, bathing, and looking into your baby's eyes. All these things help to strengthen the bond between you and baby. Newborns see best at close range – they can see your face only if it is 20-40 cm away. Let your baby stare at your face and memorize your face. This helps with bonding. If they make any cooing sounds, this is your baby communicating with you.

Your partner can bond with the baby by undertaking all the activities mentioned above. The more time you spend with your baby, the stronger the bond will become. You can also bond as a family by spending time with your partner, baby, and other children you may have. Spending time as a family makes your family relationship stronger. The baby needs to know that you are there for its needs and it needs to be able to trust you.

This bonding sets up your child for good emotional health in the future. It teaches the child what a healthy relationship with another human being is. Do not ignore your baby or its needs. You are the parent and this baby is your responsibility. Show the baby that you are a responsible, loving, dependent, and caring parent. Remember, **you cannot spoil a baby by loving it too much.** If you have any concerns about taking care of your baby's needs make sure you see your doctor.

Motherhood

Becoming a mother is a new and exciting experience. It is a new role that you will adapt to in time. Do not expect that on day one you will just fit right into the motherhood role. You need to adjust to your new role. Don't forget that **it will get easier with time**! This is just a transition period so that you can learn what your baby needs, and your baby can learn how to live in this new world.

I hope this book helps you as you embark on your journey that is motherhood. I wish you and your little one the best! Enjoy motherhood and welcome to the club!

Resources

Caring for Yourself

Mayo Clinic. Labour, Delivery, Postpartum Care".
https://www.mayoclinic.org/healthy-lifestyle/labor-and-delivery/basics/labor-and-delivery/hlv-20049465. 2017

American Pregnancy Association. "Care After a C-section".
http://americanpregnancy.org/labor-and-birth/cesarean-aftercare/.
2017.

BabyCenter. "Postpartum Hemorrhoids".
https://www.babycenter.com/0_postpartum-hemorrhoids_11708.bc. 2017

Turawa EB, Musekiwa A, Rohwer AC. "Interventions for treating postpartum constipation". *Cochrane Database of Systematic Reviews* 2014, Issue 9. Art. No.: CD010273. DOI: 10.1002/14651858.CD010273.pub2.

Spencer, J."Management of Mastitis in Breastfeeding Women".*Am Fam Physician.* 2008 Sep 15;78(6):727-731.

Goel R, Abzug JM. de Quervain's tenosynovitis: a review of the rehabilitative options. *Hand (New York, NY).* 2015;10(1):1-5. doi:10.1007/s11552-014-9649-3.

What to Expect. "Postpartum Back Pain".
https://www.whattoexpect.com/pregnancy/symptoms-and-solutions/postpartum-bachache.aspx. 2017

Ablove, R. Prevalence of carpal tunnel syndrome in pregnant women.WMJ. 2009 Jul;108(4):194-6.

Goldberg G. Maternal nutrition in pregnancy and the first postnatal year--2. After the birth. J Fam Health Care. 2005;15(5):137-8, 140.

Bane, SM. Postpartum Exercise and Lactation. Clin Obstet Gynecol. 2015 Dec;58(4):885-92. doi: 10.1097/GRF.0000000000000143.

McLintock C,et al. Recommendations for the diagnosis and treatment of deep venous thrombosis and pulmonary embolism in pregnancy and the postpartum period. Aust N Z J Obstet Gynaecol. 2012 Feb;52(1):14-22. doi: 10.1111/j.1479-828X.2011.01361.x. Epub 2011 Oct 6.

Stella CL, et al. Postpartum headache: is your work-up complete? Am J Obstet Gynecol. 2007 Apr;196(4):318.e1-7.

Pearlstein T, et al. Postpartum depression.Am J Obstet Gynecol. 2009 Apr;200(4):357-64. doi: 10.1016/j.ajog.2008.11.033.

Sit, D, et al. A Review of Postpartum Psychosis. Journal of women's health (2002). 2006;15(4):352-368. doi:10.1089/jwh.2006.15.352.

Leeman LM, Rogers RG. Sex after childbirth: postpartum sexual function. Obstet Gynecol. 2012 Mar;119(3):647-55. doi: 10.1097/AOG.0b013e3182479611.

Feeding

Stuebe A. The Risks of Not Breastfeeding for Mothers and Infants. Reviews in Obstetrics and Gynecology. 2009;2(4):222-231.

Hoddinott P, Tappin D, Wright C. Breast feeding. BMJ : British Medical Journal. 2008;336(7649):881-887. doi:10.1136/bmj.39521.566296.BE.

Martin CR, Ling P-R, Blackburn GL. Review of Infant Feeding: Key Features of Breast Milk and Infant Formula. Nutrients. 2016;8(5):279. doi:10.3390/nu8050279.

McKechnie AC, Eglash A. Nipple Shields: A Review of the Literature. Breastfeeding Medicine. 2010;5(6):309-314.

Alexander JM· et al. Randomised controlled trial of breast shells and Hoffman's exercises for inverted and non-protractile nipples. BMJ. 1992 Apr 18;304(6833):1030-2.

Black, A. Breastfeeding the premature infant and nursing implications. Adv Neonatal Care. 2012 Feb;12(1):10-1. doi: 10.1097/ANC.0b013e3182425ad6.

Shloim, N. et al. Looking for cues - infant communication of hunger and satiation during milk feeding. Appetite. 2017 Jan 1;108:74-82. doi: 10.1016/j.appet.2016.09.020. Epub 2016 Sep 17.

International Breastfeeding Centre. Videos. http://ibconline.ca/breastfeeding-videos-english/. 2017.

Sleeping

Allen KA. Promoting and Protecting Infant Sleep. Advances in neonatal care : official journal of the National Association of Neonatal Nurses. 2012;12(5):288-291. doi:10.1097/ANC.0b013e3182653899.

Tikotzky L, et al.Sleep and physical growth in infants during the first 6 months. J Sleep Res. 2010;19:103–10.

Resources

Burnham MM, et al. Nighttime sleep-wake patterns and self-soothing from birth to one year of age: a longitudinal intervention study. Journal of child psychology and psychiatry, and allied disciplines. 2002;43(6):713-725.

Canadian Pediatric Society. Creating a safe sleep environment for your baby. Paediatrics & Child Health. 2004;9(9):665-666.

Changing, Bathing, & Skin

Prasad, HR, et al. Diaper dermatitis--an overview. Indian J Pediatr. 2003 Aug;70(8):635-7.

Bozic, D. Santos, J. Newborn circumcision: Caring for your child at home after the procedure. http://www.aboutkidshealth.ca/En/HealthAZ/DevelopmentalStages/MaternalandNewborn01month/Pages/Circumcision-Caring-for-Your-Child-at-Home-After-the-Procedure.aspx. 2016.

BabyCenter. Caring for Your Newborn's Umbilical Cord Stump. https://www.babycenter.com/0_caring-for-your-newborns-umbilical-cord-stump_127.bc. 2017.

Crying

Johnson, J. et al. Infantile Colic: Recognition and Treatment. Am Fam Physician. 2015 Oct 1;92(7):577-82.

Barr, R. The normal crying curve: what do we really know? Dev Med Child Neurol. 1990 Apr;32(4):356-62.

Spaide R, et al. Shaken Baby Syndrome. Am Fam Physician. 1990 Apr;41(4):1145-52.

Additional Resources

- Baby Center Canada - http://www.babycenter.ca/
- What to Expect when You Are Expecting - http://www.whattoexpect.com
- Kids Health.org - http://kidshealth.org/
- Caring for Kids - http://www.caringforkids.cps.ca/ (Site by Canadian Pediatrics Society)
- Immunizations in Canada - http://www.phac-aspc.gc.ca/naci-ccni/index-eng.php (Site by NACI - National Advisory Committee on Immunization)
- Dr. Jack Newman, Leading Canadian Pediatrician - http://www.breastfeedinginc.ca/
- Rourke Baby Record - http://www.rourkebabyrecord.ca/ (developed by Dr. Leslie Rourke, Canadian Family Doctor)

- Purple Crying -
  http://www.purplecrying.info/
- BestStart Ontario – Breastfeeding Guide -
  http://www.beststart.org/
- Canadian Mental Health Association CMHA -
  http://www.cmha.ca/

Other Resources

- Department stores offer free gifts if you register your baby shower
- You can call baby product companies for free samples
- Sign-up for newsletters/clubs on baby product websites and they will send you free samples and/or coupons
- Diaper companies offer collection of points for free gifts

Community Resources

- Your Doctor!

- Your local Public Health Unit

- Your local Hospital

- Ask your doctor for information on other community and additional resources

About the Author

Dr. Magbule Doko is a Family Physician practising in Ontario, Canada. She is an Adjunct Professor at the Schulich School of Medicine & Dentistry at the University of Western Ontario. She has published many stories in Narrative Medicine. She is a mother, wife, sister, daughter, teacher, writer, and doctor.

Checklist

Please find the checklist from *The Essentials* Chapter. Feel free to tear it out and use it as a checklist when you are preparing for your baby to come.

Essential Baby Clothing

[ ] Short Sleeve Onesies – 10
[ ] Long Sleeve Onesies – 10
[ ] Pyjamas – 10
[ ] Pyjama Sack – 1
[ ] Pants – 10
[ ] Sweaters – 10
[ ] Hats – 2
[ ] Hand Mittens – 3
[ ] Socks – 5
[ ] Swaddle Blanket – 4
[ ] Blanket – 2
[ ] Baby Laundry Basket
[ ] Baby Memory Box and/or Book

Essential Changing Items

[ ] 1 Box Newborn Diapers
[ ] 1 Box Size 1 Diapers
[ ] Baby Wipes
[ ] Diaper Cream – large and small container
[ ] Baby Changing Pad
[ ] Diaper Light
[ ] Diaper Trash
[ ] Small Bottle with Laundry Detergent

Essential Bathing Items

[ ] Baby bathtub
[ ] Baby Shampoo/Body Wash
[ ] Baby Towel
[ ] Small Jug for Rinsing
[ ] Bath Thermometer

Essential Feeding Items

[ ] Burping Towels – 10
[ ] Bibs – 10
[ ] Bottles
[ ] Formula

Essential Equipment

[ ] Stroller
[ ] Car Seat +/- Car Seat Base
[ ] Crib + Crib Mattress
[ ] Crib Fitted Sheet & Crib Waterproof Sheet
[ ] High Chair
[ ] Baby Monitor

Essential Medical Items

[ ] Thermometer
[ ] Infants acetaminophen and/or ibuprofen
[ ] Antiseptic
[ ] Bandages
[ ] Antibiotic cream
[ ] Vitamin D Infant Drops

Essential Miscellaneous Items

[   ] Memory Book
[   ] Tissue Box
[   ] Small waste basket
[   ] Pacifier – 4
[   ] Baby Grooming Kit
[   ] Nightlight
[   ] Hypoallergenic Laundry & Dishwasher Supplies
[   ] Baby Diaper/Travel Bag

Essential Baby Diaper Bag Items

[   ] Clothing – 2 changes of clothing, 1 pyjama set, 1
        pair of socks and hand mittens, 1 hat
[   ] Diapers
[   ] Diaper Disposal Bags
[   ] Portable baby changing pad
[   ] Diaper wipes
[   ] Diaper Cream
[   ] Small bottle of Baby Wash
[   ] Burp towels and Bibs
[   ] Pacifier
[   ] Bottle
[   ] Formula
[   ] Extra Tissue
[   ] Antibiotic cream, bandages, acetaminophen or
        ibuprofen for infants

Essentials for You

[ ] 2-3 week supply Sanitary Pads
[ ] Prenatal Vitamins
[ ] Acetaminophen and Ibuprofen
[ ] Stool Softener
[ ] Nursing Bra – 2
[ ] Nursing Pads
[ ] Lanolin cream
[ ] Nursing Pillow
[ ] Breast Pump
[ ] Breastmilk Storage Bags
[ ] Ice pack

Essential Things to Do Before Baby Comes

[ ] Organize and wash baby clothes
[ ] Sterilize Bottles
[ ] Spring Cleaning
[ ] Finish House to Do List
[ ] Crib Assembly
[ ] Car Seat Base Installation
[ ] Room Setup
[ ] Charge Camcorder and Camera and Clear Storage
[ ] Book Couple Time!
[ ] Check the Maternity Benefits Paperwork
[ ] Look into CPR/First Aid Courses & updating
    Legal documents & Health Insurance

Hospital Essentials for Baby

[ ] Short Sleeve Onesies, Long Sleeve Onesies, Pyjamas, Socks, Hand Mittens, Hat
[ ] Baby Going Home Outfit
[ ] 4 Swaddle Blankets and 1 Blanket
[ ] Diapers, Diaper Cream, Wipes

Hospital Essentials for You

[ ] Change of clothing, pyjamas, slippers, going home outfit, sleep eye mask
[ ] Personal Hygiene items – shampoo, hairbrush, toothbrush, toothpaste, sanitary pads, body soap, makeup, lip balm, hand lotion
[ ] Nursing Pillow, Nursing Pads, Breast Pumps, Lanolin cream
[ ] Pillow and Blanket
[ ] Camera, Camcorder, Phone, Laptop and chargers
[ ] Snacks

Hospital Essentials for Partner/Birth-Partner

[ ] Change of Clothing, Pyjamas
[ ] Personal Hygiene items
[ ] Pillow and blanket
[ ] Phone, laptop and chargers
[ ] Snacks, Book, Magazine

And Of Course, Don't Forget:

[ ] *Becoming a Mother: The First Six Weeks* Book!

14930290R00127